MANY VILLAGES RAISED
CHARLIE PRATT

MANHATTAN COLLEGE GRAD '55
FOUR TIME NATIONAL TRACK CHAMPION

A Memoir

CHARLIE PRATT

Published by Charlie Pratt | Printed by Lighting Source

2013 Lightning Source Printing

Photos in "The Village of Manhattan College" provided courtesy of Manhattan College

Photos in "The Army as a Village" provided courtesy of the U.S. Army

Published in the United States by Charlie Pratt

ISBN 978-09886521-0-1
eBOOK ISBN 978-0-9886521-1-8
Printed in the United States of America

Book design by Jackie Schlindwein

CharliePrattVillages@gmail.com

To Miss Mildred Deal, whose invitation to our sixth grade class to join the track club piqued my interest in the sport of track and field.

I am also grateful to mentors Dr. Geissinger and Mr. Beers, who guided me inside the school system.

To Mr. Arnold Taylor, a Hall of Fame track star alumnus from Palmyra High School. He pointed me out to Mr. George Eastment, track coach of Manhattan College. His influence helped me get a track scholarship to Manhattan College.

ACKNOWLEDGMENTS

Dreams often become a reality with help of a person or persons. Marcia Cornish my assistant took a bunch of handwritten pages and turned them into a book.

Many thanks to Amy Ovsiew for editing my work.

Thank you for your generous support Fred Marro, Esq. class of '78 Manhattan College and to Mary Lenti.

To SF Hochman, thank you for sharing your unbelievable talent.

CONTENTS

I'm going to be somebody!"

As I walked by a vacant lot at the corner of Market and Front Streets in the small Delaware River town of Palmyra, my attention was drawn to a curly-headed little boy sitting on a curb. The lot had been turned into a playground by boys playing in the dirt, pitching horseshoes and quoits, and playing catch.

The little boy, sitting to the side, seemingly lost in thought, muttered to himself, "I'm going to be somebody."

An amazing statement coming from such a young child. That child's name was Charles Arthur Pratt.

That incident happened over 70 years ago in the town where I was born, the same town I live in 90 years later – Palmyra. Over the years, I witnessed that prophetic statement from the mouth of a small child coming true.

I knew several generations of his family. We called his father's father Uncle Jack. His father was Charlie. His mother's mother was Mrs. Cephas. His mother Mary was Mrs. Pratt. I know his brothers, sister and cousins. Many were legendary athletes.

That warm summer day long ago, little Charles Arthur Pratt made a challenge to himself. That challenge led him to an illustrious career in track and field and education and made him a man who has made a difference in the lives of many people from all walks of life, all over the world.

Now he has reached a point in the journey where he takes pause to pay homage and genuflect before all the kind and generous people who have helped and shaped him – family and friends from Palmyra; athletes he met in his career in track and field, in high school, college and countries around the world; classmates and teachers at Manhattan College in New York. While serving in the U.S. Army, he won the national decathlon title in 1957 and put Palmyra on the map the next year that victory led to the Amateur Athletic Union hosting its national championship at Palmyra High School's stadium.

Readers, you are in for a treat. In this book, Charles Arthur chronicles his journey, his experiences and his encounters with people whom he has touched and the people who have touched him.

I personally know many of the men and women in this book and I can truly say Charles Arthur has chronicled the history of a small South Jersey town, bringing to life authentic and vivid memories of what it was like to live in a community of people in a close knit village many years ago. His anecdotes are filled with warmth and humor as he shares the tears and the cheers and support from family – biological and extended. He captures the villages that raised a child and helped him become a success, be it a village of many or a village of one.

His inspiring stories laced with profound and deep gratitude for the people in his life are motivation for the youth from towns all over America to "be somebody." This book is an important testament to what it was like to be young, gifted and black in the United States of America.

"I am going to be somebody." A little boy's dream came true.

Charles Arthur Pratt has made an excellent pass of the baton. Enjoy.

- JOHN EMERSON WASHINGTON SR.

Palmyra, NJ - September 2011

Whenever I return to visit my hometown of Palmyra New Jersey, one topic seems to come up in most conversations. For the over-fifty age group that topic is growing up in Palmyra.

Most would agree that growing up in Palmyra was a wonderful experience. Most shared the feeling that our community was one big family. Many families were linked by blood. Those not, were often treated as such. Whether by accident or design, the elders in the community created a warm family environment.

Who were these people? They ranged from males who drank their liquids covered by a brown paper bag on the corner, men who would be considered "real characters", to others were great role models and mentors. These men with varied backgrounds had one thing in common. They would do whatever necessary to protect the people in the community and the community itself. The women in the community shared a slightly similar profile; however, the women were largely responsible for the "one big family feeling" shared within the community. Years later we are still talking about some of these people. What a challenge for us. Will people still be talking about us and how we enriched their lives long after we have passed on?

Years ago, when I first heard the phrase "It takes a village to raise a child", I was intrigued by it. Politicians, social scientists, and even some ordinary folks found comfort in using the phrase but some were using it to further their own agenda. Who could find fault with the idea of a group of people raising a child? I was captivated with the phrase even though I had some doubts about the concept. Words and phrases sometimes sound good, but their application may be lacking in sincerity and substance. Some folks said the idea, had roots in Africa. With my limited knowledge of the phrase I started creating a picture in my mind of a village. At first I pictured a group of older folks sitting around in conversation discussing how best to help a child or children. Perhaps they might have talked about ways of creating an environment that would give a child the best chance of having a good life. The more I thought of the concept of a village helping a child, scenes of my childhood surfaced. There were similarities between my picture of a village and my real childhood.

As a grownup, I began to realize that there were individual groups and institutions that qualified as a "village. My idea of a "village" gradually changed dramatically in comparison to my first concept. I was then convinced that I was raised within my new broader interpretation of "village". My "village" has included all the folks and institutions throughout my life who have enriched my life and continues to do so.

My life has been enriched when people make me the focus of their goodness and when people help to create a good environment, whether at work, at church, or at a social event. My life has been enriched even though I may not have been the center of their action! People are our greatest natural resource. The beauty and innocence of people is that they may be part of a village and not recognize it. I could walk into a group of people and say, "thanks for raising me". Hopefully they would understand what I mean. I am a wealthy person. My richness is not in money though. My wealth comes from the abundance of good people who have crossed my path. I hope this book is a way of sharing my wealth with others. There is a song we sing in church, St. Paul UAME in Palmyra, that includes the following words. "When I look back over my life… I can say that I've been truly blessed, I have a testimony"… This book is my testimony.

Another song that we sing in church led me to take on this, the biggest challenge in my life. Part of the song follows.

I said I wasn't gonna tell nobody, but I

Couldn't keep it to myself

Oh, I couldn't keep it to myself

Oh I couldn't keep it to myself

I said I wasn't gonna tell nobody, but I

Couldn't keep it to myself what the Lord has done for me

The Village of

PALMYRA

Palmyra, New Jersey, is a small town bordering the Delaware River, the river that separates New Jersey and Pennsylvania.

Growing up, I looked at Palmyra as three separate communities. There was that community on the other side of those dreaded railroad tracks. This area, by tradition, was off limits to minorities in terms of housing and socialization. Somehow we knew as a person of color where to go and not to go. The other two communities were divided by social restraints. There was that part of Palmyra we called Uptown, which housed most of the stores and businesses. Then there was the area called West Palmyra, where the people of color lived. Though this area was highly integrated, people of color were confined to this area in terms of housing and social interaction.

This four by eight-block area of Palmyra became our sanctuary, a place where we felt comfortable. In my formative years, however, I had two major concerns about Palmyra. Even as a youngster, I had the feeling that our neighborhood was considered to be on the "wrong side of the tracks." When I started going to the movies, I saw scenes that portrayed people living on the "wrong side of the tracks" and these scenes only deepened my concern. To this day, I still wonder who decides which side of the tracks is the "right" or "wrong" side. Could the high school and stadium, the beautiful riverfront, and wonderful people in our neighborhood really be living on the "wrong side of the tracks"? My second childhood concern was the labeling of our community as West Palmyra. For me, "West Palmyra" took on another characterization. West Palmyra was the place where "those people" live. I hated that phrase. Years later I found that apparently others may have shared my sentiment, such as Mrs. Edna Washington Webb, one of our distinguished seniors in Palmyra. Our area was a wonderful place to spend the growing up years and the label detracted from that.

What made our neighborhood special? Beyond the people, there were tangible and intangible aspects of the neighborhood that made people feel good. As you walked around the streets, you would see modest but well-kept homes. Empty lots became playgrounds with fruit-bearing trees, mostly apples and pears. Grape arbors were in abundance, too. Children didn't have to go home for lunch because it was all around them. In our home, there was no such thing as a sit-down lunch.

Empty lots were also a source of joy for older citizens. Our elders brought a little culture to the area. Some played croquet on the corner of Fourth and Arch Streets. It looked like a fun game reserved for older folks. (In fact, I bought a croquet set last year.) Other empty lots were the sites for seniors engaged in fierce but friendly competitions of horseshoes and quoits. It was fun to watch them. (I recently bought some horseshoes, also.)

In time, the need for new housing took away most of the empty lots. Many people who grew up in Palmyra wanted to stay in the neighborhood to raise their children. The need for new houses began to dot the landscape.

The croquet field was one of the early casualties. The loss of the game of croquet left us with only one so-called "cultural activity." On Fourth and Markets Streets was a tennis court I vaguely recall people playing on. People with my pedigree didn't play tennis, though. Any thought of having a future tennis champion among my peer group was slim to none. The tennis court fell in disrepair and remained empty for a number of years.

With the scarcity of empty lots, our play areas were the fields between Market Street and Route 73. What was great about these fields was the abundance of blackberry bushes. Many days our mother would send us out to pick blackberries. She never received a complaint out of any of us because we knew we were in for a treat. Her blackberry dumplings were very special.

In one of the many conversations in my visits to Palmyra, someone lamented about the disappearance of grape arbors in the neighborhood. That topic led people to talk about families that made wine due to the abundance of grapes, wild cherries and berries. Most of the wine was consumed by family and friends within a couple of days. Some of the wine was buried in the wine maker's yard to hide from others. My Uncle Buss Pratt, I believe, made blackberry wine. If my memory serves me right, Grandmom Pratt would take a little taste of his wine on occasion – according to her, only for "medicinal purposes." Grandmom was way ahead of those who drink wine for health reasons. I believe you, Grandmom. That's why I drink it!

While the men were busy making wine, the women were canning fruits and veggies. The process of sterilizing empty jars in hot water and return the full jars back to the hot water required both resolve and patience. I know because our mom included us in the work. Thanks to the women, food was always available, even in hard times. I don't believe anyone in the neighborhood went to bed hungry.

Hard work in our community was a given among the adults. This work ethic was passed down to the young people. We were encouraged to work hard at a very young age. Throughout the neighborhood were some young entrepreneurs, both boys and girls, who collected paper, rags, glass bottles and iron. Mr. George Cherry and Mr. Lloyd Smith (aka junk men) would buy these items from us. Those two men were thought to be among the wealthiest in our part of town.

Somewhere around the age of seven or eight, my friend Billy King and I had our own business. Since Billy was older by two months, I guess he was the boss. We both lived on Jefferson Street and sold our items to Mr. George, who lived two houses away. Sometime after selling our items to Mr. George, some of those items were back in our possession in a day or two. How they got there, I don't know (maybe my boss knew). Mr. George's son, (George) and his daughter (Barbara), both knew, but they never told their dad. Their dad probably knew too.

In those days, there was no such thing as receiving an allowance from parents. When my children, Chuck and Jennifer, asked for an allowance, I told them I never knew what the word meant, and I still don't. The absence of a family allowance was not our only motivation for wanting to work, though. There was a sense of pride in earning money.

When adults sensed this quality in us, they gave us little jobs or chores to earn money. When I got a little older, my neighbor Mr. Andrew Byron would give me the job of cleaning his basement. Four or five days later, he would tell me his basement needed to be cleaned again. I would remind him that I had cleaned the basement several days ago, but he would say: "That's alright, clean it again."

My son in-law, Wayne Irons is a throwback to the old days. He has helped young men by giving them jobs around his house. He would go to Palmyra from Voorhees and pick up my grand-nephew Malik and his friend Marcus. Marcus was a good worker. Wayne also used young men in his neighborhood.

As we got a little older, we realized we could buy our own candy, cookies and sodas. We had several choices. First there was Mr. George's store, then later it was Prisco's or Rosie's store. All served the community, but in different ways: If parents were low on money and needed groceries, they went to Prisco's. No problem. They pulled out a book and recorded the amount of your purchase. At the end of the week, parents paid the bill. The Prisco family was a real asset to our neighborhood. They were also the first family in the neighborhood to have a television. They shared their 12 inch black and white TV with us. When important shows or events (such as heavy weight championship fights) were scheduled, they turned the TV toward their windows on Third Street so that we were able to stand outside and watch the event.

If we wanted to satisfy our lust for food, we went to Rosie's. She made the best Italian hoagie in the world. No one could just stop with the hoagie, though – her famous potato chips were a must. They didn't come pre-packaged. They came to Rosie in a big tin can, from which she would fill a small brown bag with chips. Within a few minutes, the brown bag started to change color from the grease from the potato chips. Rosie's chips were so good, a young lady named Audrey Jean and her friends tried to sneak chips in their pocketbooks to eat during church service at Evergreen Baptist Church.

Now what about a soda and Jewish pickle? The pocketbook or wallet dictated how far down the menu a person could afford. Knowing that Rosie's menu would satisfy all hunger pains was a great motivator for working and having your own money. It was torture to watch the guys profiling on the corner eating their food.

The other great motivator for having money was clothes. Guys wanted to be fashion plates. The girls in the same age group were way ahead of them in dressing, especially for holidays and Sunday church. The unofficial Easter Parade around the streets was something to see.

New Easter outfits were almost required in our neighborhood. The guys didn't have to go to 5th Avenue in New York, however, to buy their clothes. We went where the hipsters meet, South Street, in Philly. Sorry to Sandra, my wife, for stealing the song from the group you sang with, The Orlons. They made this song popular, back in the day. "Where do all the hippies meet? South Street, South Street." Tailor-made pants cost $14.95 or $15.95.

On Saturday nights, we dressed in what we called "nice casual," meaning a nice pair of trousers, sport coat, and a nice sport shirt. Sundays were special. That was the day we got dressed up in a suit, white shirt and tie. At some point, colored dress shirts replaced the white shirt. Blue, pink and yellow shirts were in vogue. No doubt, we were ready for the runway … but no calls came our way. With no calls to model clothes, our peer group turned our attention to high school sports.

With the high school stadium so close, we were exposed to both high school and semi-pro football. The stadium was built under a program called the Works Progress Administration (WPA), a program initially established in 1935 and later redesigned in 1939 and transferred to the Federal Works Agency. Under this program, work was offered to the unemployed in a wide variety of programs, including highway and building construction, slum clearance, restoration and rural rehabilitation.

Many of our fathers were part of the workforce that built the stadium. I remember walking three blocks almost every day to watch my father work on the stadium. Years later, he told me that he once told his fellow workers that one day his sons would perform in the stadium.

Knowing my father, I can believe he said it. He was either a soothsayer or a great storyteller — maybe a combination of both.

Without a doubt, the stadium was one of Palmyra's cherished jewels. For years, the stadium was the site of all the South Jersey Group and Burlington County Track and Field Championships. Years later, the stadium was the site of a national event.

In addition, the Red Devils, a semi-pro football team, played Friday night football under portable lights. The names of some of the Red Devils players are still in my memory bank, though I have forgotten many. I remember the following: Uncle Buss, Josey Peditto, the Sacca brothers, Pete Heisler, Tee-Wee Flournoy, Reds Conwell and Ike DeShields.

Palmyra had a history of being a great sports town. Ed Conwell, with a number of state championships in track, continued his success at New York University where he became a member of the 1948 Olympic Team in London. However, travel to Europe at that time was by boat. With a pre-existing health condition, Ed's health was affected on the boat trip. His dream of competing in the Olympics was dashed because of his illness.

However, Ed's four National Championships in the 60-yard dash speak for themselves, especially when you win those championships at the famed Madison Square Garden in New York City. Ed returned to his hometown of Riverton (all locations in this book are in New Jersey unless otherwise noted), to finish out his life. His career work with the Philadelphia Department of Recreation was well recognized in the city and beyond. Many of Philadelphia's outstanding basketball players got their early start in Mr. Conwell's recreation center, including Wilt Chamberlain and John Chaney, the now-retired Temple basketball coach. I don't know whether Guy Rodgers the great basketball player at Temple and several pro basketball teams were part of the group influence by Mr. Conwell. When I was a part-time toll collector at the Tacony-Palmyra Bridge, Guy Rodgers recognized me and would come through my lane. It was a joy to see him and briefly talk with him.

In September 1947, I started my freshman year of high school. Thanks to the accomplishments of Ed Conwell and Tee-Wee Flournoy, I was encouraged to do something with my life. I joined the track team but struggled.

Between my freshman year and the start of my sophomore year, something good happened to me. Dr. John Geissinger,

Superintendent of Schools, approached me after a track meet. He asked whether I had given any thought about attending college. He talked with me about scholarships available in sports.

I don't remember how I responded, but I was glad he was interested in me. He told me that he would review my school records and make sure I was taking the right courses for college.

When I returned to school for my sophomore year, I found that he had done what he had promised. I was scheduled for the academic courses required for college. After that chance meeting with Dr. Geissinger, I wondered if he was partially blind. Didn't he see this kid who weighed less than 100 pounds finish last in every race in his freshman year?

This giant of a man was not deterred. Dr. Geissinger remained a mentor to me. Several years after college, I received an award at Rutgers University. Rocky Cancelleri, ex-football coach, athletic director and superintendant of schools in nearby Riverside had nominated me for an achievement award. At my request, Dr. Geissinger presented the award. It was good to see him again. We talked about his time in Palmyra and the times he had come to see me compete in Madison Square Garden.

Mr. Prentice Beers, my football coach and Algebra II teacher, also took a real interest in me. I didn't go out for football until my junior year because I was too small. Even then, I played on the junior varsity team. Some of my friends and my cousin Baldy played on the varsity team. If a player didn't make the varsity team he didn't get a varsity uniform, so I had to pay or jump the fence to see my friends play. Of course, I jumped the fence. What a humbling experience to watch the varsity team.

Over the summer before my senior year, I received a letter from Coach Beers welcoming me to the varsity football team. I didn't realize that a letter was sent to all football candidates. Nevertheless, I felt special to receive the letter.

With only one year of varsity football experience, Coach Beers wanted me to consider a football scholarship at Syracuse University. His college football coach at Muhlenberg, Ben Schwartzwalder, had become the head football coach at Syracuse University.

Weighing less than 150 pounds, I said thanks but no thanks. Instead, I graduated from high school and received a track scholarship to college. I was one of the few black males in Palmyra that got lucky. Thanks to my track coach, Mr. Matt Curtis, who entered me in the track meets that gave me great exposure like the Penn Relays and the Meet of Champions in addition to the State Championships at Rutgers University.

People in Palmyra continue to heap praise on the town because of how we grew up. No argument from me. However, I think the town had one glaring blemish in those days. That blemish was the school system. Some of the lower grades were segregated before I started school. My fifth grade class was in a large room with all black students in fifth and sixth grades. I still have visions of our teacher, a black lady named Mrs. Ruth Baylor, walking from one side of the room to the other. During that time she was not allowed to teach white students.

Mrs. Baylor was determined to teach us those basic skills expected of fifth and sixth graders. This teacher exhibited dignity and class. She also recognized the importance of how we presented ourselves to others and how people perceived us. On occasion she would talk to us about our appearance and personal hygiene. Mrs. Baylor was a caring person and a good educator.

There was another woman, Miss Mildred Deal, who showed some interest in our class. Miss Deal started a track club and invited our sixth grade class to join. I remember Miss Deal teaching my cousin James Hinson and me how to run over at the stadium. She was instrumental in piquing my interest in the sport of track and field.

No doubt, there were some wonderful people and fine educators in the school system; however wonderful people and fine educators are not always synonymous. Did those good people have academic expectations for minority students? Early on, minority students were often perceived to be doing well based on their performance on the playground, the gym and music classes. As a parent, when I went to see about my son in his early grades, some teachers in his school system (not Palmyra) were quick to talk about how good he was in gym or music class. I would have to remind them that I was more interested in how he was doing in math, science and English.

To me, black males appeared to suffer more than black females in the early grades in the Palmyra school system. A high percentage of them had to repeat one or two grades. I almost didn't graduate from eighth grade because of my music class. I refused to sing "Ole Black Joe" or "Ole Black Sambo" or something similar. Those songs were offensive to people of color. I was sent to the cloak room for refusing to sing. Thanks to my parents, I did graduate and participate in the ceremony; however, my name was left out of the program.

Those of us who entered high school, both males and females, had few curriculum choices unless our IQ was very high. Most of us landed in general, clerical or vocational agriculture courses.

Did minority students suffer because of low expectations by educators? Was academic and career guidance offered to minorities? If so, was it tainted with bias? Were academically talented females encouraged to seek careers beyond that of a housewife or secretary? For the black males, was their success measured only by their performance on the football field, the track, or the basketball court? I don't know. Sometimes it seemed that way.

In the late 1950's, I spoke to a black audience about my experience as a young teacher. I told them their children's education was a shared responsibility between them and the school system. When parents, regardless of color or ethnic origin, send their children to school with a healthy respect towards the teachers, good things can happen. Participation in school activities and programs is the only way to know what is going on in the school system. Personal conferences with your child's teacher are important. Be prepared to discuss your expectation for your child and your expectation of the school system. Proper dress and manners can only help a child's image.

Some folks got mad at me for that comment. No one can tell me how to dress my child for school, some people said. Recently, Dr. William (Bill) Cosby spoke to a group and probably said something similar to what I said years ago. From what I heard, he didn't please everyone, either. For years, people said I look like Bill Cosby – that's wrong, though, since I'm older … Bill Cosby looks like me. If that's true about what he said, it's good to know we have something in common besides looks.

I was fortunate to have mentors like Dr. Geissinger and Mr. Beers, but also to have someone outside of the school system to help me. Mr. Arnold Taylor, a Hall of Fame track star alumnus from Palmyra High School, moved to New York when I was in grade school. He never lost his interest in track. He would go to see his cousin Ed (Reds) Conwell compete at Madison Square Garden. At the Garden, he became a fan of Manhattan College's track program. During one of the meets, Mr. Taylor spoke to Mr. George Eastment, the track coach of Manhattan College, about me. He was instrumental in me getting a track scholarship at Manhattan College.

Mr. Taylor followed my career at Manhattan College. When Barbara and George Cherry came to New York to see me compete in an afternoon track meet, Mr. Taylor had a surprise for us. After the track meet, he took us to a club in Harlem called the Red Rooster. Before we entered the club he said we might see baseball great Willie Mays. Sure enough, he was there.

Mr. Taylor came to my college graduation. The night before, he drove from New York to Palmyra and brought my mother and two grandmothers back with him. For these ladies, it was their first and only trip to New York.

Reflecting on my school experience, I realized I was blessed to go from Jefferson Street in Palmyra to 242nd St in New York (the location of Manhattan College).

Thanks to villagers like Dr. Geissinger and Mr. Taylor, unknown to each other, the opportunity for higher education became a reality for me. I am grateful for growing up in Palmyra, a town with a high school and track team. For a country boy, my thoughts of having access to the biggest and best city in the world, New York City was daunting. Palmyra was just the place some Pennsylvanians had to pass through on their way to the Jersey Shore.

When Mr. Andrew Byron took me to the train station in Philadelphia for my trip to New York, I was ready to take a bite out of the Big Apple. I had one big suit case full of clothes, and a few other things that didn't require a suitcase: the memories of the people and events that made this trip possible.

To read more about the memories of these people and events, please go to the appendix at the end of the book.

The Village of

MANHATTAN COLLEGE

Ken Bantum, Coach Eastment and Lou Jones

Joe Schatzle, Jack O'Connell, Lindy Remigino, and Bob Carty
World's Fastest Relay Team, 1951 and 1952

O'Connell, Schatzle, Remigino and Carty. Those four names were Manhattan College to me.

In my senior year in high school, I ran in the world famous Penn Relays in Philadelphia. For the third year in a row, our high school relay team finished almost last in our event. All was not lost, however, because I enjoyed watching the college relay teams. One of my favorite events was the 440 relay. Each member of the relay team would run 110 yards to complete the one lap race around the track. This race requires both speed and precise baton passing. The first day of competition, I watched the trials of the 440 relay. I watched four guys in what I thought were ugly green uniforms win their trial race. I was impressed. Later that day, they duplicated their success in the trials for the 880 relay. Those four guys represented Manhattan College from Riverdale, New York.

The next day, the finals of the Relay Championships of America were about to begin. I couldn't wait. I wanted to see those guys in those ugly green uniforms. When they called the teams to take their positions for the 440 relay final, Jack O'Connell was the leadoff man for Manhattan College. At the sound of the starter's gun, Jack ran the first 110 yards and passed the baton to Joe Schatzle, who passed the baton to Lindy Remigino. At this point in the race, I couldn't tell who was leading. After Lindy passed the baton to anchorman Bob Carty, I still didn't know who was winning until the last 50 yards of the race. There was no question what team would be the winner, Manhattan College. Bob Carty the anchorman kept the lead given to him by Jack, Joe and Lindy. Later that day Manhattan College won their second relay Championship of America in the 880 relay.

I was brave for cheering for Manhattan College while sitting in a stadium full of fans of Morgan State, a predominantly black college that had enjoyed great success at the Penn Relays. Wonder what they thought of seeing me rooting for a team with three white and one black member?

Until that weekend at the Penn Relays, Manhattan College was almost unknown to me. On occasions at the movies, they would show sports from Madison Square Garden in New York I remember seeing, Joe Ciancibella from Manhattan College in one of those sports segments. Joe was easy to recognize in the 60 yard dash. Parts of his track shoes in the back were cut away – no one knew why.

After the Penn Relays, my focus was on the South Jersey and State Track and Field Championships. I had some success in those Championships as a junior. I won the 120 yard high hurdles and 220 yard low hurdles championships and finished second in the long jump competition. Could I repeat as a senior?

Yes, and I did. I won every competition I entered, starting with the first dual meet through the State Championships. After the State Championships, I was offered a track scholarship to Manhattan College. I didn't consider other scholarships. I couldn't believe I was going to the same college with that great relay team. I guess those green uniforms really didn't look so bad after all.

I didn't know anything about Manhattan College. I didn't care where it was located or what it looked like. If it was good enough for a team I called the Magnificent Four, it was good enough for me.

Several days after high school graduation, Mr. George Eastment, track coach at Manhattan College, invited my dad and me to visit the campus and meet with him for the first time. During that meeting, Coach Eastment and Brother Abdon Lewis from the faculty talked about the college's academic program. After listening to both of them, I realized this independent Catholic institution offered more than just a great relay team.

After the meeting, Coach Eastment gave us a short tour of the campus. While touring, Coach Eastment saw Joe Schatzle, a member of that great relay team, and pointed toward him. Then he talked about the success of the 440 and 880 relay team. He also pointed out Vern Dixon, who I had read about in Jet Magazine so I knew something about him. According to the Magazine this gifted student from Bishop Laughlin High School in Brooklyn, New York was also a gifted athlete who would attend Manhattan College on an academic scholarship. When I looked at Vern, I realized that life is not always fair. He was a gifted student, a gifted athlete, and handsome. For a short moment I wondered if I was in the wrong place. When the meeting had ended, I left looking forward to returning to the school in September.

When I returned to the College in September, it wasn't that easy in terms of travel.

I had to take a train from Philadelphia to New York City, then two different subways to get to 242nd Street the location of the college in Riverdale, New York. After that, I had to walk up a hill to the campus.

With my bag safely in my dorm room, I was anxious to meet my roommate and the guys who would be our neighbors for the next four years. I was ready for dorm life. With very little activity in the dorm, I got ready for the Freshman Orientation Program in the auditorium. I don't remember everything that was said in the orientation, but this I do remember. The Brother who spoke to us said, "Look at the person on your left and look at the person on your right. One of you may not be here after the first semester." The Christian Brothers were dedicated and clearly placed a high priority on the standards that made Manhattan College a first class institution.

Outside, before freshman orientation, I met a family of three – a mother, father and son. The mother approached me and asked if I was alone. When I said yes, she put her arm in my arm and told me I was "not alone anymore." I later found out these were the parents of L. Jay Oliva. Their concern assured me that I was in the right place. L. Jay Oliva became one of Manhattan College's distinguished graduates.

When I finally met my roommate, James (Jim) Patrick Lake from Iselin, New Jersey I sensed that for whatever awaited us, together we would prevail. Jim was an All-State basketball player on scholarship from Woodbridge High School in Woodbridge, New Jersey. Like most basketball players, Jim couldn't pass a gym without wanting to start a pickup game.

After settling in the dorm, Jim and other basketball players headed for the gym. I went to see these guys play. What I saw was amazing. My knowledge of basketball was very limited but I could recognize talent. Watching Jim in that pick-up game, I saw real talent. His quickness and jumping ability was at a level I have never seen before. I don't remember all the guys who participated in that game but I suspect the following; Dan Martinsen, Bob Murphy, Angie Lombardo, Ed O'Conner, Bob Otten, Jack Pascal, Jerry Paulson and John O'Connor.

Cahill, Carroll, Kawaters, Claire, Miller, Johnson, Otten, O'Connor, Kellogg, Doran, Pascal, Ryan, Lake, Hunt, Norton, McGowan, O'Haire   *1952-53*

BASKETBALL TEAM

Carty-Dixon-Jones-Ferraro - 11 Laps Mile –relay World-record

THE 1953 OUTDOOR CHAMPIONS
Manhattan College

First Row: (l. to R) Frank Gaffney, Henry Bereuk, John O'Connell, Lindy Remigino, Ron Lucas, Marriott Dowden and James Enright. *Second Row:* Mgr. Robert McVey. *Third Row:* (L. to R) Bob Audolensky, Ray Drobinski, Frank Egan, Vincent Galli, Don Driscoll, Charles Santaga, Gerald Zurlini and Coach George T. Eastment. *Fourth Row:* (L. to R) Vern Dixon, Bill Schertzer, Lou Jones, Charles Pratt, Wally Pinza, Ron Ferraro, Bill Baker and Trainer John Johnson. *Fifth Row:* (L. to R) John Pavacic, Al Larsen, Joe Schutzle, Steve Dillon, Mike Martin, Bob Kubic and Manager Bill Murphy. *Back Row:* (l. to R) Mgr. Tom Flannagan, John McCarthy, Ed Pellegrini and Mgr. Bob Reiss.

My roommate was a key member of the basketball team for four years. At one of our Block "M" Banquets for the sports teams, our speaker was a former New York Yankee and a member of the professional Baseball Hall of Fame. In his talk, he mentioned how much he enjoyed watching Jim play at Madison Square Garden.

Jim and I became good friends and I would go home with him on weekends when possible. Unfortunately, I had track practice most Saturdays starting early in September that kept me in

Charlie Pratt, Jack Pascal, Bro. John Muller

the dorms on weekends. When I went home with Jim, however, his family treated me as one of them. Most of the family simply called me Pratt. They could have called me anything as long as Jim's mom had that big pot of beans and rice on the stove. Jim's mother, Rose, was from Trinidad and most of her cooking had that wonderful West Indian flair. Jim's dad, James, was a mason contractor and was as handsome as Clark Gable. I don't know how old he was, but he looked better than both of us.

In addition to my roommate, there were some good guys staying in the dorm. Ben Benson, who roomed next to us, was and continues to be a class act. Years later, during retirement, Ben volunteered his time to promote Manhattan College. Ben remains my best link to the college.

When track practice started early in September, I really wasn't prepared. Track practice in high school started in March. In high school there was no indoor track season. At the first practice, Coach Eastment talked about the indoor season; the Senior Metropolitan Championships were scheduled for December 26. This Championship was open to anyone in the New York metropolitan area. Coach also talked about our dual meet against the United States Military Academy at West Point. When he started talking about the Intercollegiate Association of Amateur Athletes of America (IC4A's) Championships, I realized he placed a high priority on team success over individual success.

At practice, I began to meet some of the track guys. Seeing and meeting these gifted athletes was a great experience. Their success and the team's success put some pressure on me. Because I was at Manhattan on a track scholarship, I was consumed by being successful. The thought of having to win was continually on my mind.

For the hurdlers and sprinters, our early workouts consisted of jogging a little more than a mile and running wind sprints at Van Courtland Park. I had never jogged more than a half mile. It took some time before I felt comfortable jogging the distance. After a month or so, our workout changed. Our new workouts included jogging the famous cross-country course – that meant jogging four or five miles. Pure torture for me.

Van Courtland Park, where we trained, was several blocks from the college. It is the site of many important cross country championships. One day, I jogged the cross country course with one of my heroes from that relay team, Bob Carty. I fell, coming down one of the rocky hills and hurt my big toe on the right foot. I got up like nothing happened – of course I had to look tough in front of my hero. After I graduated I would joke with Bob that my big toe still hurt from time to time and "blamed" him for the fall. I reminded him of my "pain" until his passing. The "pain" is still there, along with the memories of how I got the pain and the joy of jogging with the great Bob Carty.

Did Coach Eastment forget, or did he just not care that I was a hurdler and not a distance runner? During the indoor season, my longest race would be 60 yards. It should take me less than eight seconds to do that. Why was I jogging four miles? I guess if you want to run with the big boys, you have to do what the big boys do.

One day I was running wind sprints with Lindy Remigino, another member of that famed relay team. I was in awe of him. This was early in the year and I thought he was running pretty hard. After a few sprints, I asked him why he was running so hard this early in the year. His reply: "This is Olympic year." That meant nothing to me. For Lindy, however, it represented one of his cherished goals. He achieved his goal by winning the most coveted race in the 1952 Olympics, the 100 meter dash, in Helsinki, Finland. Upon his return to the college campus, he was our hero and inspiration. His victory in the Olympics also raised Manhattan College's profile to an international level.

Track practice can sometimes wear on you, especially when your competition is still weeks away. When my spirits were low, all I had to do was to visit the trainer's room. In that room was a very special person –John (Doc) Johnson, the athletic trainer for Manhattan's sports teams. He also held a similar position with the New York Giants football team. You could always talk with him. His rub downs not only cured your aches and pains, they gave you relief from the mental stress of training. Sometimes I would go to sleep on John's training table.

John continued to treat me when I was still competing after college. Whenever Vern Dixon and I returned to the college for an activity, we would visit John first. After serving the College for 50 years, he retired in 2003. However, John was still with the New York Giants when they won the Super Bowl several years later. John Johnson still remains one of Manhattan's prized possessions.

Two other gentlemen partnered with John Johnson to serve the college's athletes; the equipment manager and the medical doctor. Charlie Cummings, the equipment manager, was always pleasant and more than accommodating. The other gentleman (that's a stretch) was Dr. Francis Sweeney. Fire and brimstone is the only way to describe Dr. Sweeney. What came out of his mouth during sporting events, especially at basketball games, made the Brothers blush.

At basketball games, John Johnson's assignment was to keep Dr. Sweeney from getting to the referees. John probably needed a trainer himself because his arms must have been sore from re-straining Dr. Sweeney. Like John Johnson, Dr. Sweeney also had a similar position with the New York Giants football team. The team of John Johnson and Dr. Sweeney contributed greatly to the success of the college's sports program.

I met a number of committed people like Dr. Francis Sweeney and John Johnson at Manhattan College. That commitment was present throughout the college campus. Everything seemed great, except on weekends. The majority of students were commuters who returned to their homes each day. There were no classes on Saturday. Most of the small number of students living in the dorms lived close enough to go home every weekend. The athletes who stayed in the dorms, even those who had practice on Saturday, would go home Friday and come back in the morning and then return home again after practice.

I didn't have that luxury because I lived too far away, even if I had a car. Using public transportation would have taken me more than four hours to get home. All that was good about the college, sadly, couldn't fill the void of a nearly-deserted campus on the weekends. Many weekends I ate meals by myself, walked around campus by myself. If I had any imagination, I could have looked at the dorm as my big mansion for the weekend. Many bedrooms and bathrooms and a couple of game rooms, access to a large dining room a gym close by, a swimming pool with nice clean clear water. All of that and a great view of New York City. The absence of a great imagination left me in a state of loneliness. When Monday morning came the campus came alive again and so did I.

After the start of the indoor track season the day after Christmas, there was a good chance that my weekends wouldn't be so lonely. Most track meets were held on Friday or Saturday nights.

The track team, within two months, had three important meets: the Metropolitan Collegiate Championships, the dual meet with the United States Military Academy at West Point and the IC4A Championship.

After more than three months of training, the track and field athletes were ready for competition. The Senior Metropolitan Championships on December 26 would give us a chance to measure our progress.

At the meet, my tie for first place with Foster Green in the 70 yard high hurdles was encouraging. This track meet was a preview of future competition. As a freshman I could be competing against upperclassmen, national and Olympic champions.

The rivalry between Manhattan College and the Military Academy took on a life of its own. It was like the Yankees against the Red Sox, or the Celtics against the Lakers.

The thought of competing at West Point brings back memories of the glory days of West Point football with the likes of Glenn Davis and Felix Doc Blanchard, and Coach Earl Red Blake. The Academy was among the best college football teams in America in the early 1940's. Davis and Blanchard both earned three-time all American status. With their different running styles, they became known as Mr. Inside and Mr. Outside. Blanchard, Mr. Inside – with his size and power, ran the football straight ahead. Davis, Mr. Outside with his speed, ran away from the middle of the defensive line. The names of Felix "Doc" Blanchard and Glenn Davis were synonymous with greatness.

The dual meet with West Point was the highlight of my sports career to date. When I got on the team bus for our trip to West Point, I realized I had come a long way from Jefferson Street in Palmyra. When our bus went through the gate to enter the campus, it felt like I was in an environment separate from anything I had seen before. Reality set in when Coach Eastment gave his pep talk. Coach Eastment wanted to win this dual meet against the Academy. No one knew this better than the team.

Our first activity was lunch, in that large and unique mess hall. When the cadets marched in, they were a picture of discipline. The discipline displayed by the Cadets made me proud of them. Some of us realized that, we would last about one week at the Academy. Lunch was great, but runners and jumpers had to curb their appetites, because you can't run and jump on a full stomach. To maintain their strength the weight men enjoyed a full lunch. After lunch, we headed to the heated field house, the site for the track meet. Again, I thought that life wasn't fair. The Cadets had this well-equipped great field house to train in. We had to train all winter, outside in the cold, for the indoor track season. West Point had a well balanced team, but our team won most of the competitions. The upperclassmen performed at a high level, as expected. It was the guys who finished second and third in their events, however, that earned important points. These were the guys who earned points in events beyond their comfort level.

That was Coach Eastment's philosophy: be prepared to compete in an event that's not your specialty if it helps the team. Teammates admired the guys who competed in events outside of their training and comfort level. After the meet, we returned to the mess hall for dinner. This time the runners and jumpers could enjoy a full meal. During dinner time, scores of the day's sports competition were announced over the Public address system. Sometimes I failed to hear the scores of Manhattan's victory.

After the West Point meet, Coach Eastment started preparing us for the indoor IC4A Championships. Back to our outdoor training sessions. Sometimes we had to shovel snow off the wooden board track before we could practice. As bad as it was for us, it was worse for Coach Eastment during practice. Because of class schedules for the athletes, Coach Eastment was at practice between three and four hours a day, much longer than the athletes.

As expected, we won the IC4A Championships. Those who were expected to perform well, did so. However, performance by lesser-known teammates made the difference between winning and losing a valuable contribution to the victory. My fourth place finish in the hurdles and fifth place in the long jump was not overlooked. The same could be said about fellow freshman Al Larsen for his contribution in the weight event. We were treated like we had won our individual events. Coach Eastment acknowledged third, fourth and fifth place finishes as much as he did for first and second finishes. There was joy following our team victory.

My joy was brief, however. I had to return to an empty dormitory. The ride on two different subways and the following walk to the campus in cold weather made me an unhappy camper. That experience taught me that winning in sports is not a cure for everything. That was a good lesson for me that later became a part of my mental portfolio.

In trying to find some social interaction on the campus, I went to several of the school's Tea Dances (I don't want the home boys to know this!). The Tea Dances were held on Sunday afternoons from 3-5 p.m. in the school's library. Sipping tea in a fancy cup was a challenge – I was always concerned that my pinky finger was in the wrong position. No one at the dances looked like me.

The Tea Dances were very different than the dances at the Meadowbrook back home – there, you got a full body work out doing the fast dances. You could easily build up a sweat with all that moving around. Most of the music live or recorded, was meant for fast dancing. The music at the Tea Dances was for slow dancing.

But I never got a chance to dance at the Tea Dances – and when one of the Brothers asked me why, I told him and he said he would look at the nearby all-girl's college and see if any minority girls were there that would attend the Tea Dances. No luck. The Brother politely suggested that I forget the Tea Dances.

When I had concerns related to school or track, I would go to Coach Easement's office. One of his best talents was his ability to make you forget your problems or concerns. He would immediately tell me about a phone call he had just received from home or an acquaintance. The calls always brought bad news. After hearing his story, either I forgot why I was there or I realized my concerns were not that important. I would leave after some small talk. It took this naïve country boy several visits before I realized that I had been outsmarted by the coach. On occasion, Coach Eastment would tell me something that would make me feel good. Once he told me that he saw Jackie Robinson and that

Jackie sent his regards to me. I really wanted to believe that my first hero knew I existed. Mr. Robinson did come to some of the track meets in Madison Square Garden. Maybe he did know me. Coach wouldn't mislead a country boy, would he?

The coming of spring brought an air of optimism. The track team was primed for a successful outdoor season. The Penn Relays in Philadelphia was high on the coach's priority list.

I would be able to visit home several times after the indoor season. Each time I came home I could expect two things. My cousin, Charles John (Bozo) Pratt, would let me use his car and give me some money. Also, my brothers, Petey and Merrill, would give me money. Even if I didn't see them, I would check my coat pockets or travel bag after getting back to school and money was sure to be there.

Coming into the Penn Relays, I was a little disappointed, but not too much. I had a leg injury and couldn't compete. If I were healthy, Coach might have put me on the freshmen mile relay team. That meant I would have had to run the quarter mile, a distance I hated with a passion.

What a difference a year makes. I got to see O'Connell, Schatzle, Remingino and Carty in their pretty green uniforms successfully defend their two championships of American titles. Last year they were unknown to me – now they were my team-mates. The Magnificent Four were primed to defend their titles in the Los Angeles Coliseum. The sprint relay team successfully defended their titles. The mile relay team finished second in strong competition.

Afterwards, the track team won an outdoor dual meet at

West Point. With team victories at West Point, the Metropolitan Collegiate Championship and the IC4A Championship, we had a good year.

As the school year came to an end, I had a big decision to make. Did I want to transfer to a college closer to home? Campus life hadn't changed. However, the more I thought about leaving Manhattan College, the more I thought about those wonderful people I met this year. How could I give that up? Maybe with a car I would have some flexibility on the weekends.

When I got home for the summer, I had two goals: get a job and buy a car. In pursuit of a car, I worked three jobs: a full-time position at Campbell Soup in Camden, meeting the early morning mail trains for the post office and working at a gas station. After saving $500, I had my eyes on a 1946 maroon Ford that cost $695. When I told my brother Petey about the car, he asked how much more I needed in order to buy the car. He went upstairs, gave me $200 and told me to get my car. I did.

When I returned to college in my car, I was ready for the Big Apple. My car was shining and my white wall tires were freshly painted – in those days, poor folks bought black tires and painted them white, a weekly chore.

Within a few days of returning to school, something happened that may have changed the course of my life. Lou Jones, a teammate one year ahead of me, knew my ambivalent feeling about returning to Manhattan College. One day after track practice he said to me, "Charlie, you will be going home with me on the weekends."

The joy I felt that first weekend with Lou Jones carried over for the next three years. From then on, I spent much of my weekends with the Jones family.

Another bit of good news came from my coach. Coach Eastment informed me that I would be a member of the 440 and 880 relay team. Bob Carty, the anchor man, had graduated and left an opening.

How proud I was to be a part of the team of O'Connell, Pratt, Schatzle, and Remigino? We had great practices. Our baton exchanges were flawless. Could this group continue the success of the past two years?

The talent was there, but it wasn't meant to be. The team was scheduled to compete in three relay carnivals: the Seton Hall Relays, the Penn Relays and the Coliseum Relays. At the Seton Hall Relays, a member of the sprint team got spiked during the race and couldn't finish. His sub for the Penn Relays also got hurt during the race and couldn't finish. Would the team still get an invitation to compete in the Coliseum Relay in Los Angeles?

We had two weeks to get everyone well. With Manhattan's previous success in California, we got the invitation: both the sprint team and the mile relay team were invited to compete. This would be my first time on a plane and my last chance to run with Jack O'Connell, Joe Schatzle and Lindy Remigino.

When we arrived in California, we were greeted as if we were the World Champion New York Yankees. When the teams went over to the practice area, I was amazed at the respect we received. Coaches and athletes from high profile colleges were very accommodating. The Manhattan College alumni from the area treated us as if we were royalty. A reception at a beautiful home of one of the Manhattan grads in an upscale neighborhood made me think again life is not always fair.

The night before the competition, athletes, coaches and officials were invited to a lavish banquet at the Helm's Foundation Hall of Fame Pavilion, an outside facility. Athletes from all areas of the country were present at the banquet. The program, food and camaraderie was a great experience.

When we returned to our hotel, there was an atmosphere of joy coupled with guarded anticipation about tomorrow's events. For some of us, tomorrow's competition would be our biggest competition to date. After some small talk in the hotel lobby we returned to our rooms in hopes of getting some sleep. Wally Pina, a member of the mile relay team was my roommate.

Everything came crashing down with one phone call after midnight. That call informed us that one of our teammates was sick with food poisoning. After that call, the word was out that several other guys were sick. By morning, the sprint team was wiped out, including me. Some were hospitalized. My chance to run with the sprint team was over.

Luckily for them, the mile relay team wasn't affected like the sprint team. They had enough somewhat healthy bodies to compete in the relay carnival. Wally Pina, Vern Dixon, Lou Jones and a substitute made up the mile relay team. The performance of the mile relay team took some sting out the misfortune that plagued the trip.

With outstanding performances from Vern Dixon and Lou Jones, plus Wally Pina's solid lead off leg, the team finished second. The second place was not a surprise. The past two years they were over shadowed by the tremendous success of O'Connell, Schatzle, Remigino and Carty. However, there was some drama after the finish of the mile relay race. Vern Dixon was injured at the Penn Relays and had limited time to prepare for his race. His 46.8 relay leg helped Lou Jones to secure second place. Vern got sick after his race and fell out in the infield. I went over to him. I could see that he was out of it, he asked me to get a Priest. He was afraid and I was afraid for him when he asked for a Priest. After receiving medical attention, Vern was okay.

The following day, most of us were healthy enough to fly back to New York. The plane ride back to New York was full of disappointment. My last chance to run with Jack, Joe and Lindy was gone forever. That disappointment continues to keep me captive. I have tried to rationalize and reconcile the events that plagued this team. The team I once named The Magnificent Four didn't have the name of Pratt as part of that group. Maybe it was meant to be that way.

After California and for the next two years, I was part of a team that enjoyed great success. In four years, Coach Eastment's teams won eight IC4A Championships. They also won eight Metropolitan Collegiate Championships (indoors and outdoors). The IC4A Championship included cross country victories. As a senior, I was on two teams that won two Championships of American Titles at the Penn Relays. The shuttle hurdle team of Brendan Dooley, Ken Bantum, Lou Knight and Charlie Pratt won gold watches. The 880 relay team won gold watches with performances from Arthur Cassell, Charlie Pratt, Richard Simmons and Lenny Moore.

I returned to California as a senior to compete in the National Collegiate Championships. Tom Courtney from Fordham University and I went out together and were roommates. When our plane landed in California, members of the Manhattan alumni were there to greet me. Manhattan pride was on display during my week in California. Manhattan people are a special breed.

When I entered the Coliseum for the first day of competition, I saw Jim Lake, my roommate, and Joe Schatzle in the stadium. They returned the next day to see me finish second to Milt Campbell in the high hurdles and first in the 220 yard low hurdles. Tom Courtney won the 880 yard Championships. After the meet was over, the Manhattan alumni gave me a celebration party.

Years after graduation, I recognized that Manhattan College was an important village in my life. I left as a winner, not because I won a few races, but because of the Manhattan College community. The mission of the college was to educate students, not create superstar athletes.

The athletic staff, faculty and administration were on that same page. The Christian Brothers had real expectations of their students.

If Manhattan College had a blemish, it only became obvious when Jim and I sought help on job opportunities after we graduated. We were sent to a company in New York City. Soon after they gave us a math test, we were told that we were not what they were looking for. We never sat down and talked with anyone during that visit. We felt like it was more of a 'window dressing.' We knew a sham when we witnessed one. Back on campus there was no follow-up on the trip to the company.

Vern Dixon, one of Manhattan's prized honor students, advised me to go into the Army for two years and consider a career in education, where there were opportunities for people of color. Thanks to him many times for that advice. I had no regrets, even after I heard that minority students in competing colleges with degrees in business received help to enter the business world. During my long association with Vern Dixon, he made it clear he wasn't privy to the contacts that some of his classmates received in the School of Business. The fact that he served on Manhattan Colleges Board of Trustees speaks for his true feelings about the college. He was proud to be a graduate from Manhattan College. Manhattan's blemish could not cancel out four years of what Manhattan College had to offer. Nor could it block the path to success.

After graduation, I made rare visits to the campus. One of the best experiences in returning was the inauguration ceremony for the Sports Hall of Fame. This program was more than honoring former athletes. It brought together people who hadn't seen one another since graduation. Thanks to those who laid the ground work for the Sports Hall of Fame, including Jack Powers, class of 1958 and athletic director at the time.

Over the years, the Hall of Fame Program blossomed under the leadership of Bob Byrnes, class of 1968 and athletic director. The Hall of Fame selection committee should also be commended for their commitment. Their philosophy of honoring team success in addition to individual success was a big plus. As individuals, that group would stand little chance of being elected in the Sports Hall of Fame.

At the Hall of Fame Programs, I sense the honorees look at themselves as members of one big team, Team Manhattan College. That atmosphere of oneness is also evident at the dinner tables. I see a good mixture of athletes, families and supporters of the Hall of Fame together.

In addition to the teammates already mentioned, please go to the appendix at the end of the book to read more about the people and events at Manhattan College that also enriched my life.

After college, I started to participate in events sponsored by the school and various alumni groups. One group I enjoy participating in is the alumni group of Philadelphia. Tom Muldoon, class of 1962, was the host of most of these events or activities. They were first-class outings. Tom made sure that everyone was important to the group.

At one of the functions in Philadelphia, I was treated to a pleasant surprise when a certain couple entered the eatery. The female reminded me of Dr. Sweeney, Manhattan College's sports doctor. Sure enough, it was his daughter, Sheila, and her husband, Thomas Conlon, a 1955 graduate. Sheila was the spitting image of her father and she sounded just like him. Thank heaven; her choice of words didn't match that of her father. If it had, the Quakers of Philadelphia would have invited all of us to leave the city. It was a joy meeting Sheila. The few times I've seen her and Thomas, it was like I was in the company of her father. The last time I saw Sheila, she shared this story about her father. Back in her college days she needed a new dress for a formal affair. She went to her dad for the money. He asked her if her date was a Manhattan College student. She said no, he went to Fordham.

He told her to "wear one of your old dresses in the closet" – With Dr. Sweeney, there was no compromising on his loyalty to Manhattan College.

There were two other alumni events that caught my attention. Every year, the college alumni have a golf outing in May. When the invitation came in the mail, into the waste basket it went. Why would I want to play golf with the country club set? Why embarrass myself with my raggedy game?

My position didn't change for several years. Then, one year I got a call from Mr. Good Guy, Ben Benson. My pride went out the window and I accepted an invitation to play in my first golf outing in north Jersey. I played in a foursome with Tom Lindgren, a track teammate, and two guys who played basketball, Bob Otten and Jack Pascal. What a great time, great food and fellowship.

I was hooked and looked forward to playing with these guys each year. Jack Pascal was always one of my favorite people in college. He looked like he belonged in Hollywood. His collection of sweaters in college caught my eye and he was gracious enough to let me borrow some when I went home. Tom Lindgren and Bob Otten made me feel comfortable in spite of my lack of talent.

After a few years, the golf outing was moved to Westchester County, New York, a two and half to three hour drive for me. The first time I played in New York, both the weather and my golf game were bad. The ride home at night was an experience. It was a challenge to get to the big George Washington Bridge. Once I found the Bridge, the next challenge was to take the right roads that would lead to the New Jersey Turnpike. You don't want to know where I ended up sometimes! When I was safely on the New Jersey Turnpike, I would stop at the first service area for a cup of coffee to calm my nerves and thank the Lord I was back in New Jersey.

The following year, the weather was even worse. It rained all day, it was cold and my golf game ... let's not talk about it. My back was already hurting when I arrived at the golf course. I wasn't able to play the first two holes. I needed to walk and loosen up.

Somewhere around the fifteenth hole, the group started talking about how it wouldn't be long before we could take a hot shower and enjoy a good meal. Mind you, we were playing at an upscale country club. When we finished playing, we rushed to the locker room only to hear someone say there was no hot water. No, I thought, that can't be true at this first class golf facility.

Sadly, it was true – guys were showering in cold water. To prove my manliness, I showered like the water was 80 degrees ... for two or three minutes. After a good meal and a short program, I then had to face that unwanted challenge of getting to the New Jersey Turnpike. I managed to do it but it wasn't easy in the rain. I got behind a big truck on one of the New York Parkway's and followed it through the toll lane – an EZ Pass Lane. Of course, I didn't have EZ Pass access.

After the golf outings, people would ask about my trip to New York. I had the nerve to tell people I had a great time. I think Ben Benson put something in my wine glass at the outing for me to say that.

Then, in 2003, I received a travel brochure from the college about an alumni trip to Sorrento, Italy the following spring. Thoughts of my one day trip to Sorrento in 1956 (thanks to my track career) piqued my interest in returning to that beautiful city. Without knowing anyone going on the trip, I made plans to go and meet the traveling group at the airport the day of departure. I wasn't concerned about who would be on the trip. If the trip was sponsored through Manhattan College, that was good enough for me. I met the traveling group at Kennedy Airport in New York several hours before departure. In that time, we got to know each other. Once settled in our hotel in Sorrento, each day was a new experience. The day spent in Naples and the ruins of Pompeii was one of the highlights of the trip. Even traveling by bus to interested sites wasn't free of excitement. Every day the bus had to travel around the mountains on narrow roads and low guard rails. When I looked out the bus window, the boats in the Bay of Naples looked like toys. I sat in a seat away from the guard rails. It was a great trip. Thanks to Robert Fink, class of 1957, the chairman of the Alumni Travel Committee, and his wife Mary.

The following people were part of the traveling group to Italy.

Albert and Joyce Buettner	Frank and Regina Cuomo
John Flynn	Janet Hannon
Dorothy Heiskell	Joseph and Elizabeth McIntyre
Dominic McParland	Josephs and Julie Merlin
Michael and Anne Marie Morrell	Joseph Petroni, M.D.
Peter and Diane Sweeney	Wolfgang and Evelyn Stupiel
Robert and Mary Fink	Paul and Marjorie Vermaelen

Staying connected to Manhattan College has been a blessing. Manhattan College continues to attract the kind of people that makes the college a first-class institution. Returning to the college for our Class of '55 reunion was a good time for all who came together for three days in June 2010.

Thanks to Ben Benson, the class reunion committee (including James Brennan, Henry Boucher, Tom Tuffy, John Lawler and Al Larsen) and some special people on the staff (including Grace Feeney, Ellen Kiernan, Thomas Mauriello, Tom McCarthy, Kathy Muskoph and Stephen L. White), I still stay connected to the College. The following alumni in the Philadelphia area keep me apprised of alumni activities in the area: Fred Marro, Brendan Monaghan, both classes of 1978, and Tom Muldoon, class of 1962.

Alumni Trip to Sorrento, Italy

Patty and Bob English- Manhattan Class of 56

Lou Jones

and the Village of

New Rochelle, New York

Louis (Lou) Woodward Jones, III, was born, raised and educated in New Rochelle, New York. His parents and grandparents were considered middle class. His grandfather on his father's side was highly admired as a successful entrepreneur. Lou's mother came from a large family in Connecticut.

When Lou, my track teammate, first invited me to come home with him to his parents' home on weekends, I had many questions. What was I in for? What kind of town is New Rochelle? Will his parents and friends accept me?

When the time came, we left the college campus in my shiny 1946 maroon two-door Ford. Off we went; Lou navigating, me driving. I never saw so many parkways and highways between the college and the exit for New Rochelle. After leaving the parkway, the tree-lined street looked different than the streets back home. As some from Palmyra might say, you could almost smell the money. My 1946 Ford looked out of place.

Mrs. Anita Jones, Lou's mother, was home to greet us. After the introductions and some small talk, Mrs. Jones told us to take our bags upstairs to our bedroom. When we came down, she told us to visit Lou's grandparents, who lived close by. Out the back door we went. Visiting Lou's grandparents was the first thing we did every weekend, before dinner or social activities.

After our first dinner, Mrs. Jones gave us her second bit of orders. Fellows you are responsible for cleaning off the table and doing the dishes. I felt right at home. Mrs. Jones sounded like my mom and her sisters. She was a no-nonsense woman. After a few weeks, I started calling her Momma Jones. I was the new son in the house. Momma Jones would refer to me as her foster son.

Lou's father, Louis Woodward Jones Jr., was always Mr. Jones to me. Mr. Jones was an easy going, soft-spoken man. He was the picture of tranquility that made me realize that he was a special person. A father of two sons, he allowed me to have the same privileges reserved for his sons. Mr. Jones was so reserved that he never talked about his athletic career as a National Champion on the National Negro Tennis Circuit. His family also had some interest in the Pittsburgh Crawford's, a Professional Baseball Team in the Negro League. (My father played semi pro baseball, he told me about the players and teams in the Negro League.) I recognized the name, The Pittsburgh Crawford's. The first weekend in New Rochelle was a memorable one. Friday night football was my introduction to the community. High school sports were very popular in town; none more popular than Friday night football under the lights.

When Lou entered the stadium, friends and admirers gathered around him. Only three years removed from high school, Lou had been a member of the high school football team. He was part of a backfield that was considered an All-American Backfield. Lou and three other members of the football team also ran track. In his senior year the foursome won the high school mile relay Championship of America at the Penn Relays. During his freshman year at Manhattan College, Lou was one of the budding star athletes on campus.

With that résumé, it was easy to understand why Lou

received the attention he did at the football game. I enjoyed every moment under the bright lights. For many New Yorkers, the bright lights on Broadway were a source of pride. For me, the bright lights at the football game on Friday nights lit a path for a brighter future for me. The rest of that first weekend was full of activities with family and friends.

Back on campus, I saw Lou all the time, though I tried to avoid him at track practice. He was a quarter miler and I didn't trust anyone who ran over 220 yards. Knowing Coach Eastment, he might make me run on the mile relay team if he saw me training with Lou. Sometimes after summer vacation, Lou would come back to school, a few pounds overweight. It took him time to get in shape. I would make fun of him. His reply, "just wait, I'll get even." Get even, he did. When he got in shape, he looked for somebody to beat on. When he ran his series of 220's or 300's, teammates wished they were in the shower. In his senior year, he came back to school again a few pounds overweight. By this time, I was able to jog the flats (1 ½ or 2 miles). I went looking for Lou. Let's run the flats. He would look at me and laugh. When I told him I would give him a 150 yard head start, he would laugh some more. I would give him a head start, and he would take it. Again, he threatened me; "just wait until I get in shape." Sometimes I couldn't avoid him, when he was in shape we worked out together. I paid the price I had to visit John Johnson the trainer, my body was aching. Somehow, I had to get even with Lou for making me change my wardrobe. He made fun of my tailor made clothes in my freshman year. He told people, my peg pants were so tight, that I had trouble putting them on, and I had a Zoot Suit with chains in my clothes closet. None of it was true, but Lou was having fun.

Each weekend in New Rochelle was somewhat special. During the first Thanksgiving holidays with the Jones family, I met most of Lou's friends. There were a group of guys who were very special to him. They grew up together and called themselves the Morris Street Ramblers, since their elementary school and play area were located on Morris Street. It was also the place where they planned their escapades, and the site of their football field.

In Palmyra, we called our football field the "Dust Bowl." The Morris Street Gang (what used to be The Morris Street Ramblers) called their football field the "Toilet Bowl;" … yes, the "Toilet Bowl." I thought all Westchester County folks had some class – one point for Palmyra. Each year during the Thanksgiving holidays, the guys had their annual "Toilet Bowl" Football Game. Most of the guys were home from school. Some were still playing on their college football teams. After that game, I guess I was an honorary member of the group.

The following is a small sample of what the Gang did; for recreation, for fun, to amuse themselves or others; pick one, or all.

– The Gang would play war in the woods wearing military uniforms. They would fight among themselves because everybody wanted to be an Army officer.

– Bill Billups broke his arm hitching a ride on John Simmons' bike.

– John Simmons' mother was a hairdresser, John, Lou, Lindsey Liscomb, Charlie Billups, and Bill Billups raided Mrs. Simmons' supply cabinet for something to straighten their hair. They found something all right. Shortly after that, their heads and hair were burning. There was a mad dash to Mrs. Simmons' sink, where she washed hair. Some found that the toilet bowel was just what the doctor ordered. Norris Gray, who lived close by, declined the invitation to the hair party. He knew the combination of Bill Billups and John Simmons spelled trouble.

– Some of the would-be soldiers broke into Lincoln School and set off the alarms. They thought it was patriotic to set them off to signal the end of World War II.

– The following are some of the names of the guys who were the Morris Street Gang.

George Anderson	Louis Jones
Jessie Arnelle	Lindsey Liscomb
Charles Billups	Frederick Montero
William Billups (Bill)	Samuel "Sammy" Morrison
Christopher Bozwell	Clifford Brown
Arman Prudian [another adopted member]	
Donald Robertson	Donald Carew
Henry (Hank) Scott	George Chandler
John Simmons	Williams "Fuzzy" Farr
Richard Wilkins	Norris Gray
Herbet White	Melvin Holland
Dewitt Rosebrough	Jery Johnson
Clayton Riley	

From 1952 to the present time, the guys have treated me like I was always one of them. Because of Lou's status in the community of New Rochelle, the love his friends showed me was unconditional. It must be the culture of New Rochelle. The two years I spent with the Jones, I met so many wonderful people.

The Village of New Rochelle reminded me of Palmyra; one big family of caring people. My three years at Manhattan College with Lou Jones was truly a blessing to me. While he was becoming a world class athlete at Manhattan, he didn't separate himself from me. After some of the track meets at Madison Square Garden, Lou was invited to parties hosted by Olympic Champions. Lou would take the "country boy" from Palmyra with him. He liked to call me.

Lou graduated from Manhattan College in 1954, a year before me. We still saw one another at various track meets. Both of us were in the Army and training for the 1956 Olympics in Melbourne, Australia. Before that, Lou was picked to represent the United States in the 1955 Pan American Games in Mexico City. This would be his first time competing in international competition.

Though he had a great college career, this was international competition. His debut in international competition, however, was great. He won the 400 meter race in a world record time of 45.4 seconds. His first gold medal in an international competition earned him a trip to several South American countries for more races. Brazil was one of his favorite countries.

In the spring of 1956, the State Department and Amateur Athletic Union invited me to go on a Goodwill tour of West

Africa. Several countries in West Africa were gaining their independence from European countries. The State Department in Washington, D.C. wanted some track and field athletes to conduct clinics, visit schools and compete against the West African athletes.

I told Lou about the trip and he wanted to go. After a few phone calls, Lou was added to the trip roster. We were part of a group of athletes, coaches and State Department officials. Our trip to West Africa started in New York, then on to London. Once there, we transferred to a two-engine plane.

It took us two days to get to West Africa, since our plane had to refuel every three or four hours. The refueling stop in southern Spain was in a remote place. I don't remember seeing anything but sand. Our scheduled overnight stop was in Tangiers in North Africa. Some of us were crazy enough to visit the casbah in Tangiers with narrow streets full of people and shops. Young men calling me brother, look we are the same color – they would say anything to get me to buy something.

Our group was glad to get on our plane in the morning on our way to West Africa. Our group visited Serra Leone, the Gold Coast, Ghana, Liberia and Nigeria. It was great to experience these different cultures with a group of people from different parts of the States, including California, Utah, Chicago, Atlanta, Pennsylvania and New York.

When Lou and I returned from our trip, there was a big challenge waiting for us: the 1956 Olympic Trials in Los Angeles was less than two months away. Being in the Army, we were assigned to a military base in California to train for the trials. We were in a barracks with other Army athletes training for the Olympic trials. There was some serious training with one goal: to make the 1956 Olympic Team.

The night before the Olympic Trials, Lou and I stayed in a hotel close to the Coliseum, the site of the Olympic trials. Lou's race was scheduled for the first day of the trials. My race was scheduled for the second day of competition. That night, Lou had trouble sleeping. He took the mattress off the bed and put it on the floor and tried to sleep on it there, but that didn't work. Back to the bed with the mattress didn't work, either. He even tried to take the mattress off the bed and sleep on the box spring, but that didn't work. So it was back to the regular bed. I watched the whole thing and didn't dare say anything. It was almost funny … but Lou's hopes and dreams lie less than 24 hours away.

Apparently, Lou's strategy worked, he made the Olympic Team. I can only imagine the joy Lou felt when he won his race. He wasn't satisfied with just winning – his time of 45.2 seconds for the 400 meters was a new world record. Later in the year, Lou won his second gold medal in the 1956 Olympics. He was part of the winning 4 x 400 relay team anchored by Charlie Jenkins, the gold medalist in the 400 meter dash.

Shortly after the Olympics, Lou married Vivian Jones. Vivian grew up in Scarsdale, New York, one of the most affluent communities in the United States. When I first met Miss Jones, I could tell she was exposed to some of the finer things in life. Her walk, talk and clothes represented her exposure to an upscale environment. Thanks to the Morris Street Gang, I was a part of Lou's bachelor's party. The party was in the basement of

Norris Gray's parents' house; several houses from the Jones' house (thank heaven).

The wedding was beautiful. My partner in the wedding party was one of Vivian's best friends, Lenorann (Lenny) Jubilee. Lenorann was a carbon copy of Vivian Jones. The guys in Palmyra would probably label the two, part of the 500 or 600 set, high on the social registry.

After the wedding, I saw Lou once. He, Vivian, and their friends, LaRuth and Norris Gray, came to New Jersey to see the house we built. Our guests were impressed with the custom-made house. The house idea came about after the Decathlon in Palmyra when I was talking to Mr. Mumford Ruffin, my mother's friend. He heard I wanted to build a California style house. He said he had always wanted to build and if I was willing to help him he would take on the project. I said yes, knowing that my sports career would be over. Mr. Ruffin made it clear before I went to the architect that he was the brains and I was the brawn. He would decide how the house would be built and materials used. Our sub-floor would be tongue and groove, nailed on an angle to better support hardwood floors. The walls would be plaster, thanks to Mr. Wilson Best and Mr. Slim Hunt, they did a great job on the walls. Sanding and staining the floors and doors was my job. Mr. Ruffin required several coats of stain and lots of sanding of the floors and doors. I made some boo boos sanding the floors. While staining the floor once, I backed myself into a corner. In one year, we built the house. Our New York guests could not believe the quality of Mr. Ruffin's work. I told them how much I learned working with Mr. Ruffin on the house. When I was helping Mr. Mumford Ruffin, Chuck and Jennifer would watch us work. They must have thought they were carpenters. When Mr. William Still (Marion Still-Buck's father), a member of the famous Still clan, was building his house across the street, Chuck and Jenni thought they would offer their services. At ages four and two, they got hammers and a few nails and went across the street to drive some nails in Mr. Still's sub floor. After telling that story to Lou and Vivian I promised them when we come to New York to see them I'll make sure that Chuck and Jenni leave their tool boxes at home.

Sometime after Vivian and Lou's visit to us in Moorestown, he called the house and invited the Pratt household to spend a weekend with them in New York. The visit with the Jones had one condition: don't come up without Prisco's sausage.

During our college days, Lou tasted my mother's spaghetti with meatballs and Prisco's sausage. It was one of Lou's favorite meals. My mother knew of our planned visit with the Jones, so she volunteered to make her special chocolate cake for the visit, as well. Off we went to New York, bearing gifts of Prisco's sausage and my mother's three-layer chocolate cake. Lou and Vivian were living in an apartment on the second floor of Vivian's parent's home in Elmsford, New York. That weekend, I got a chance to get to know Vivian's parents, Katie and Alphonso Jones. Both Lou's and Vivian's parents were gems. Vivian's dad wasn't laid-back, like Lou's dad. He would always greet me with a big hello, "Charlie Pratt." I always looked forward to seeing Vivian's parents when I went to New York.

The first weekend with the Jones' was the start of a new social lifestyle for the Pratt's. The social scene in Westchester County and New York City revolved around a ladies club that Vivian belonged called the Erudites of Westchester. The Erudites were a group of ladies who enjoyed an array of social activities. More importantly, they enjoyed each other. Once or twice a year, The Erudites would sponsor an activity. That activity could be formal, semi-formal or casual. Most of the house parties were held at Vivian and Lou's house in White Plains, (Greenbrook) New York. My favorite activity was the dances with live music. The music usually had a West Indian flair. Some of the dances were held in New York City, and some local. The dances made me forget the Tea Dances at Manhattan College. Chuck and Jenni liked the house parties. At the parties they would team up with the Jones' children; Woody, Steven and maybe Carla, and spy on the party people. Knowing Chuck, he led the charge in search for food. Jenni still talks about those parties. I think she wanted to grow up to be an Erudite.

One activity, really stands out – a cookout in July or August. It was the first and last time I went to a cookout in a black suit, white shirt and tie. This cookout was not sponsored by the Erudites but the two people hosting were Erudites.

The following are the names of the Erudites, as I recall:

Dorius Billings	Antoinette Johnson
Jean Brown	Lovely H. Billups
Vivian V. Jones	Lenoreann Jubilee
Brenda Glass Carew	Evelyn Lee
Geri Carty	Dorothy Robertson

Liz Covington	Velma Scott
Delores Garrett	Dorothy Sergeant
LaRuth Gray-Morgan	Virginia Higgs
Virginia Sledge	Anna Wilkins

Erudites

These ladies (and their significant others) from Westchester County enriched our lives. They allowed me to strengthen my bond with the Morris Street Gang. Through these relationships, I became friendly with two guys outside of the Morris Street Gang: James Jubilee and Ivan Sargeant. The breakfasts and/or lunches the day after the social events were special. Prisco's sausage and my mom's three layered chocolate cake became part of the smorgasbord.

In the early seventies, there was a change in family dynamics for both the Jones and Pratt families. I missed the social activities

Lou and Momma Jones

of the Erudites. Vivian's parents returned to North Carolina after their retirement. Vivian's parents treated me like Lou's parents had: like I was their own child. Lou continued to visit Vivian's parents in North Carolina until their passing. Those changes, however, did not affect my relationship with Lou, his parents or friends. Special events in New York or events involving the Jones family would be reason enough for Sandra, my second wife and me to visit Lou. We went to Lou's mother's 85th birthday party in New Rochelle. We looked forward to the next one, but it wasn't meant to be.

The early deaths of friends and brother, Alan took a toll on Lou. The deaths of his parents came at a time when he began to have health issues. Over time, his health condition required hospitalization and rehabilitation. He didn't want me to see him that way, but as I told him, there was nothing in our lives that bad that could break this bond between us.

I would visit Lou as often as I could. During these visits we would talk about the good ole days. One of his favorite subjects was his children, Woody (Louis IV), Steven my God Child, and his daughter, Carla. He was proud of what they had accomplished. I let him know that I was proud of their career choices and success. During one of the hospital visits, Lou asked me to take him home, to our house. How do you tell your friend who took you home, when you were in college, no? That two and a half hour drive home wasn't easy. All through Lou's sickness, Vivian Jones was there to assist their three children in his care. She helped him, when he gave his mother her eighty fifth birthday party. She also arranged a birthday party for him when he was hospitalized. Son, Steven catered the party and I came home with enough food and goodies, to last for three days. Don't tell anybody, but Vivian Jones walked around the hospital like she was the Chief Administrator. During one hospital visit, a patient had a party in their room. There was cake left in the hallway. She told me, I'll get some cake for you to take home. She did. All I could say to her, "Go Girl."

In February 2006, this great human being with two gold medals in track, could not out run death. Lou's funeral was held at St. Catherine's A.M.E. Zion Church in New Rochelle, New York, the same church we used to attend when we were in College.

I stayed in Lou's grandparents' house the night before the funeral.

The sight of old friends like Harry Bright and wife Becky, and Charlie Jenkins at the funeral brought some joy to a sad occasion. Harry Bright was our teammate on the Goodwill tour to West Africa. Charlie Jenkins was Lou's teammate on the 1956 Olympic Team. After the funeral, I spent time with some of the Morris Street Gang. Back at the family home, I spent time with Aunt Mamie Jones, Ivan Sargeant and LaRuth Gray-Morgan. I've known LaRuth almost as long as I've known the Jones family. She has always been a supporter of the Jones family. With a Doctorate in Education, Dr. LaRuth Gray-Morgan is an asset to the West Chester County Community. My bond with the Jones family and New Rochelle will continue through Lou's children, his ex-wife and his friends. Since his passing, I attended several events honoring his memory, including renaming his street from Winyah Terrace to Lou Jones Terrance. It's always great to see Lou's children and their mother.

Whenever I return to the New Rochelle area, I look foreward to seeing Hank Scott, Skip Morrison and Bill Billups, the three I knew best from the Morris Street Group. Plus Aunt Mamie Jones, Dr. Gray-Morgan, Ivan Sargeant and James Jubliee.

Years ago I remember Bill singing a song at a funeral in New Rochelle. That song was, "If I can help somebody… then my living shall not be in vain." If each town had a song that defines who they are, that song would define the Village of New Rochelle. Bill Billups has picked up Lou Jones' baton in taking care of Lou's old friend, Charlie Pratt.

Goodwill Contingent to West Africa

A greeting card from Lou that expressed the special
relationship between us

The One Man Village
MILT CAMPBELL

Milt Campbell, the 1953 National Decathlon Champion, the 1955 National Collegiate High Hurdles Champion, the 1955 National Amateur Athletic Union (AAU) High Hurdles Champion and the 1956 Olympic Decathlon Champion. A gifted athlete from Plainfield, New Jersey Milt is one of my all-time favorite athletes.

Milt has contributed to the little success I had in track and field. However, if someone asked Milt how he contributed to my success, he probably wouldn't know. After some thought, he might say – "I know. I used to beat Charlie in the high hurdles all the time" – and he would be right.

The first time I saw Milt, I was a sophomore in high school competing in the Long Branch Relays in New Jersey. Milt and his older brother Tom were part of the shuttle hurdle team that won at that event by a wide margin. The Campbell brothers were outstanding hurdlers. Both looked like they could compete against college hurdlers.

I was a member of the two mile relay team. My performance was bad, bad, bad. I can almost picture how bad I must have looked trying to run the half mile. I was desperate and trying several events after finishing last in the low hurdles in every race as a freshman.

The next time I saw Milt was at the state track meet at Rutgers University in my junior year. I entered three events; the low and high hurdles and the long jump. After failures in my freshman and sophomore years, I had some success in the hurdles and long jump as a junior. Why I switched to the high hurdles is still a mystery to me. Compared to Milt, I looked like I should be playing in a sandbox.

The high hurdles in Palmyra were made of solid wood. If I hit one, it would hit me back. Down on the cinder track I would go. Something I didn't know about the high hurdles until my senior year – the height of the high hurdles was 42 inches in New Jersey and two other states, the same height run by college hurdlers. All other states high hurdles were 39 inches. Those three inches made a difference.

In the trial heats at the state meet, I ran hard all through the races. Milt ran hard through the last hurdle, and eased up at the finish line. His times in the heats were better than mine. Thank heaven; I didn't have to run against him. He came from a Group IV school; I came from a Group I school. Both of us won the hurdles in our groups.

I finished second in the long jump. It would be a year before I saw Milt, again at the state meet. It rained all day, and after eight races and six attempts in the long jump, I won both hurdles and long jump. I was overjoyed that Palmyra High School had won their second straight state track and field championship. My joy was only enhanced when I heard that my high hurdle time was the same as Milt's time. The high hurdles had been lowered to 39 inches that year.

Two years passed before I saw Milt again. In the summer of 1953 I saw Milt compete in the National Decathlon

Championships in his hometown of Plainfield. He won that Championship. Plainfield was the site of the Championships because Milt finished second to the legendary Bob Mathias in the decathlon in the 1952 Olympics, in Helsinki, Finland. I knew Milt was good, but making the Olympic Team as a high schooler in the decathlon, a ten event competition over two days, was amazing. As I viewed the competition, I let my mind wonder. Wow it would be nice if something like this could happen to me. After the competition, thoughts of what I witnessed and the crazy thoughts I entertained were gone.

In 1955, I met Milt for the first time in California, at the National Collegiate Association of America (NCAA) Championships. Both of us were entered in the high hurdles. I was also entered in the low hurdles. Milt won the high hurdles and I finished second. Milt stopped running the low hurdles; a good move for me, as I won the 220 yard low hurdles. The Jersey guys brought both hurdle titles home to New Jersey.

During this meet, Milt and I became somewhat friendly. As much as I admired Milt, I hated losing to him; I wanted to win a National Championship in the high hurdles. After the National Collegiate Championships, we traveled together to Colorado for the National Championships. The results were similar to the National Collegiate Championships, except that I finished third to Milt in the high hurdles. I won my first National Championship in the low hurdles.

In the National Championships, it is important that you finish in the top three of your event. The top three finishers can be selected for competition in Europe or other destinations outside of the United States. My goal was to travel to Europe, where track and field was popular.

When I shared my thoughts with Milt, he told me about a 30-day trip to Jamaica. He talked about his prior visit to Jamaica after the 1952 Olympics. It wasn't a hard sell. I would be traveling with my hero, Milt Campbell. When I first saw Milt at the Long Branch Relays, I never dreamed that we would compete against each other, let alone forge a friendship. Europe had to take a back seat to Jamaica.

Lou Knight, my teammate at Manhattan College, was from Jamaica. I looked forward to seeing and competing against Lou on his own turf.

Off to Jamaica we went with a contingent of American athletes eager to compete against teams throughout the Caribbean Islands. The plane ride to Jamaica with all of those great athletes was something special. When our plane landed in Kingston, Jamaica, I was full of joy. To think, less than one year ago my college roommate, Jim Lake and I were denied service at a restaurant in Delaware. When the door of the plane opened, I saw a sea of people who looked like me. My first reaction, I don't think I will be denied service in a restaurant on this trip. A group of Jamaican athletes were at the airport to greet us, including the Jamaican Olympians who had been part of the 1600 meter relay that won the gold medal in the 1952 Olympics.

The American team included several Olympians and National Champions. Milt would be my roommate on this trip. How odd was the track fraternity back in those days. Competitors training together, traveling and eating together, coming together to form a relay team, staying together in the same hotels and some even crazy enough to become roommates during the competition.

In addition to our competitions, we had a chance to see the Kingston area and meet the people of Jamaica. Everywhere we went, the people were good to us. The nights were full of music and activity. Most nights, people played badminton.

Keith Gardner, Herb McKinley, Dr. Louis Knight

Everything about the trip was great except Milt Campbell. I finished second to Milt in every race. Lou Knight, my college team mate and native Jamaican, suffered the same fate I suffered at the legs of Milt Campbell. He finished third behind me in our battle against the big guy.

Lou now Dr. Louis Knight, a dentist introduced me to his family and friends. He exposed me to things that the average visitor would not experience.

Milt Campbell

Josh Culbreath

Milt Campbell, Bill Miller and Charlie Pratt

Harrison Dillard, Indoor 60 yard High Hurdles champion

Milt wasn't all that bad. He helped me forge a relationship with two Olympians, Andy Stanfield and Bill Miller. Andy won the 200 meter dash in the 1952 Olympics and Bill medaled in the Javelin in the same Olympics held in Helsinki Finland.

Four Jersey guys formed a sprint relay team that was successful against the Caribbean Teams. Stanfield, East Orange; Miller, Lawnside; Campbell, Plainfield; and Pratt Palmyra.

Competing in Jamaica was a new experience for me. It was the first time I competed on foreign soil. Having world-class athletes as your teammates, competing against world-class athletes from other countries, was very special. One of our teammates really stood out – a recent high school graduate, Charles Dumas. This young man from California was one of the best high jumpers in the world.

Thanks to the Jamaican Athletic Association, I was blessed by the time I spent in Jamaica.

After the Caribbean Games, Milt joined the Navy and I joined the Army. When I reported to the Army Base in San Pedro, California to train for the Olympic Trials, guess who was there? Milt Campbell. What was this sailor doing on an Army base? Turns out he was there to beat up on me again. We trained together and competed in several meets leading up to the Olympic Trials.

Finally, at the Inter-Service Meet, I beat Milt for the first time. To say he was ticked off would be an understatement. He was mad, angry, upset, disappointed; pick one or all. After ten minutes, our relationship continued as usual. Milt was still my hero. He gave me a lesson that I failed to absorb at the time. Only years later, after my career was over, did I learn the lesson: If you want to be a champion, you have to enter the battlefield thinking nobody can beat you. That was Milt's thinking, and it served him well.

Finally, the day of the Olympic Trials was upon us. Both of us qualified for the finals. Included in the finals was Jack Davis, Lee Calhoun, Joel Shankle and two-time Olympic champion Harrison Dillard. All of our dreams would be decided in 14 seconds or less. From the starting position, we waited for the sound of the starter's gun. The gun went off, not once, but twice… someone had jumped the gun. We had to start over.

The second time, with a clean start, the race was over in less than 14 seconds. After Lee Calhoun was declared the winner and Jack Davis second place, it was undecided who finished in that all-important third place. After a 40 minute review of the photo finish, Joel Shankle was third, Milt Campbell was fourth, and yours truly was fifth. The July 1956 issue of Life Magazine showed a great sequence of the finish of the hurdle race.

Milt knew he still had a great chance of making the Olympic team in the decathlon. I, on the other hand, saw my boyhood dreams come to an end in only 14 seconds. What sent me home was me. I didn't see myself as a great champion.

Milt had great success in the hurdles and was upset not making the Olympic Team in the event. He could have easily packed his bags without talking with anyone and headed straight for the decathlon trials.

Instead, the most competitive athlete that I've ever known couldn't suppress his humanity. He was concerned about me. He told me not to go home but go with him to the decathlon trials in Indiana.

"I'll enter you in the competition and teach you the events that you have no clue about". That would be the shot put, discus, javelin and the pole vault. When it comes to the last event, the 1500 meters, he told me to pray. The other five events were not totally foreign to me.

Of course I went to the decathlon trials. When you have a friendship with a person with Milt's resume, you can't say no. Whomever Milt talked with, all arrangements with regards to registration, transportation, food and housing were taken care of.

After we arrived at Wabash College in Indiana, the site of the trials, we only had a week or so to train. Milt said, the pole vault was the most challenging to learn, so we only practiced it one day to avoid injury. I was able to clear the bar at 9'6" and Milt, assured me I would jump a foot higher in competition.

Milt helped me as much as possible, but he also had to focus on his training. He was still expected to do well with very little training for 10 events. It seemed only injury could keep Milt from making the Olympic team. After all, he had finished second in the 1952 Olympic Games in the decathlon as a high schooler.

The evening before the start of the two-day 10 event competition, my roommate Milt said to me, "Charlie, I tried to help you the best I could. You're on your own now. Don't say anything or talk to me until the Trials are over. I have to make the boat." (This was a cliché for making the team before air travel.)

After the first day of competition, I don't remember how many points I had or what position I was in. Somewhere in the competition on the second day, our Army coach, Colonel Jesse Liscomb, called me aside and said if I got a good performance in the pole vault and 1500 meter race; I could make the Olympic team.

But I had no clue when it came to the pole vault. Where was future Olympic pole vault champion, Don Bragg, when I needed him? Though Milt's training had helped, and I did jump more than a foot more than my practice height, it wasn't enough. After two days of competition, Rafer Johnson finished first and Milt second. My sixth place finish kept me off the Olympic team, but I got a consolation prize, a trip to Berlin, Germany to compete in the stadium where Jessie Owens won four Gold Medals in the 1936 Olympics.

When my dreams of being an Olympian ended, I couldn't

watch the opening and closing ceremonies for the next four or five Olympic Games. I could only imagine how it felt to march with your fellow Olympians in those smart uniforms. My mentor went on to win the 1956 Olympic Decathlon Championship in Melbourne, Australia. Milt's record-breaking performance earned him a place in the Olympic Hall of Fame. His performance was only part of his versatility as an athlete.

In high school, Milt excelled in swimming, wrestling and football. When the pro football team Cleveland Browns came after the Olympic champion, he changed uniforms and became a Cleveland Brown. While watching his games, I cheered for Milt. Someone asked how I could root for him when he used to beat you all the time. But I wasn't rooting just for Milt; I was rooting because he was wearing a football uniform and not a track uniform. That meant he could never beat me again.

With Milt out the way, I hoped that some of the other hurdlers would change sports. No luck. When I competed in the 1957 National Championships in Ohio, nothing had changed. Still no gold medal in the high hurdles.

That year, I decided not to defend my national title in the low hurdles. Could I be successful in another event? I tried the 220 yard dash and failed. I didn't qualify for the finals in the 220.

Upset, I told my coach, Ed Conwell, I wanted to go home. He told me I couldn't go home feeling the way I did. So he entered me in the Decathlon Championships in Kingsburg, California, Rafer Johnson's hometown. Rafer was second to Milt in the Olympic decathlon.

My coach and I wee in disagreement. I hadn't trained for the decathlon. Coach won the battle. Off to Kingsburg I went. No Milt Campbell to worry about, but Rafer was still competing. After finishing second to Milt in the 1956 Olympics, I was sure he was primed to do well in his hometown.

I had no expectations going to California. Mr. Murl Dotson, Rafer's high school coach, met me at the bus stop in Kingsburg and took me to his house. Mr. Dotson talked about the decathlon and assured me that he would be available if I needed anything. He treated me like I was one of his athletes. When he talked about housing, he mentioned that most of the athletes would be staying in private homes. I would be staying with Mr. & Mrs. Oscar Ellberg. After some small talk, Mr. Dotson took me to the Ellberg's home. I would call their beautiful home, my home for a week. Shortly after my arrival, Mrs. Ellberg wanted to know what kinds of food I ate. As we talked, she realized we ate the same foods. I had a feeling the Ellberg's would be a great host and they were. I enjoyed walking in their neighborhood. When I walked to the town center, people would speak and wish me good luck.

Several days passed before I saw Rafer. He visited me at the Ellberg's. During the visit, Rafer informed me that he had knee problems that would limit his participation in the competition. I hope I showed Rafer some compassion, but I would be less than honest if I said I didn't welcome Rafer's situation. Still, I didn't have any expectations of winning the decathlon. After all, this would be only my second time competing in a decathlon.

After the first day of competition (the first five events), I led the competition. I had gotten off to a great start in the first event, the 100 meters. The second event, the long jump, almost sent me home. I had three jumps and fouled on the first two. The second foul still haunts me. The last jump I jogged down the runway to make sure I didn't foul.

Before the start of the second day's competition, someone delivered me a telegram in the middle of the football field. I couldn't imagine who it was from. When I opened the telegram, it said, "Good Luck, Charlie," from Palmyra resident Tom Monk Lane. Here I am, miles away from home, about to face the biggest challenge in my sports career, and someone from home had me in their thoughts. I saved that telegram for years. After the competition, I let Tom Lane and his family know how much that telegram meant to me.

Rafer's injury and Milt's good heart made it possible for me to stand on the top of the medal stand.

After the competition was over, Mr. Dotson mentioned to me that my hometown could host the 1958 National Decathlon Championships. I told him, frankly, I didn't believe my hometown would be interested. However, before I got home, Ed Conwell had already got the ball rolling about hosting the 1958 National Decathlon Championships in Palmyra. Much of the credit goes to Ed Conwell, Palmer Adams and the Rotary Club, Bob Kershaw and the Kiwanis Club. I was pleased to know that people from my neighborhood were included in the planning process.

The week before the competition, the town was anxiously waiting for the athletes to arrive, especially Rafer Johnson. Athletes were expected from all areas of the United States. The town and I were surprised when an athlete named C.K. Yang came all the way from China. He came to Palmyra with his coach, Bill Miller, from nearby Lawnside. Bill Miller and I had been teammates on the Jamaica trip. He and Coach Conwell were friends and stayed in contact through track programs.

At the end of the two-day competition, Rafer Johnson was first, C.K. Yang second, Dave Estrom third and the host athlete, me, fourth place. I had never heard of C.K. Yang and was surprised by his performance. He was technically good in all ten events. Later, I heard he was the Asian decathlon champion before coming to Palmyra. After the competition, C.K. Yang left Palmyra with Rafer Johnson and became training partners in California.

It was a great week. The town of Palmyra raised their profile to a national level and maybe as far as the country of China. Some in Palmyra say I brought the decathlon championships to Palmyra. In my heart, I know that it was really Milt Campbell who brought the championship to Palmyra. Without him, I would never been introduced to the decathlon.

One of the drawbacks in sports is that when careers are over, there are risks of losing the relationships you once had. Athletes retire to all parts of the globe. It would be some time before I saw Milt again to thank him.

When I used to call him, I would say this is the best hurdler in New Jersey calling; he couldn't talk for a few seconds because he was laughing so hard. In September 2010, my wife Sandra and I visited Milt and Linda at their home outside of Atlanta for three days. My college roommate Jim Lake and friend Marva Bell from California was also there. Jim and Milt had known each other since high school. We had a great reunion.

But it was more than a reunion for me. I was there to challenge Milt to a race. I got up in his face, all 6'3" and 230 pounds, and told him I had been training 50 years for this moment. Of course he laughed, knowing that neither of us was crazy enough to race.

Outside of my father and Uncle Buss, Jackie Robinson is my number one all-time hero. However, I never had to compete against him like I did against two of my other heroes, Milt Campbell and Harrison Dillard, the two-time Olympic Champion. I promised Milt I wouldn't tell anyone I beat him once in my career. I also beat Harrison once, and almost a second time, in my sophomore year of college at an indoor track meet at Boston Garden. I was leading Harrison before the last hurdle and when I turned around to look for him, he passed me and won the race. That event became part of history when Track and Tennis magazine ran the following:

> *"Manhattan College has a real up-and-coming hurdling star in Charles Arthur Pratt. He's been racing the nation's greatest timbertoppers in the big indoor meets and doing surprisingly well. But he still hasn't overcome his awe of them.*

> *At the Boston A.A. meet, for instance, he was so surprised to find himself leading Harrison Dillard at the third hurdle that he turned his head to see where the great champion was. Dillard then came on to beat him by a foot or so.*

> *After the race, the Olympic champion put an arm around the youngster and said, "Look, son, don't ever look around for me. Don't you worry. I'll be there!"*

In my dreams the past 50 years, I won all of my hurdle races. Milt and Harrison took turns placing second and third. That's why I am "numero uno" in my mind. No more nightmares trying to beat them both.

THE ARMY
as a Village

Two months after graduating from college in August 1955, I joined the Army and was stationed at Fort Dix for basic training. The Army base is located about 20 miles from my hometown of Palmyra.

Since I had lived with and been around males all my life, I expected Army life to be an extension of previous experiences. Shortly after I was assigned to my living quarters (barracks), I got a message over the intercom to report to the Company Commander's office. Once there, I met Lt. Kenneth Conover from Mt. Holly, a town about 25 minutes from my home. He remembered that we had competed against each other in football and track in high school and that, four years ago as required by the draft, we had taken our physicals together. After those physicals, he went to officer training school. I returned to College after spending three days at an Army hospital. My physical detected a heart murmur, a condition I've known about since eighth grade.

Lt. Conover made me feel comfortable without compromising his ability to lead the company. He put me in charge of my barracks. I had my own squad, which meant I had to be the first one up in the morning and outside to take roll call. That role had both advantages and disadvantages. However, I took my assignment seriously. I didn't want to embarrass Lt. Conover or lose the respect of the men assigned to me.

Sometime after the fifth week of the eight week training

period, my orders changed. I trained with the troops in the morning, and the afternoon free to resume training for the Olympic Trials.

As we got near the eighth week of basic training, Lt. Conover wanted the company to prepare for the first Army headquarters inspection. The top general at the headquarters would lead the inspections. Since I missed some of the training Lt. Conover and Lt. Erskine, Lt. Conover's assistant, were worried about me. In a previous company inspection, I didn't perform up to par. I almost took off my nose while moving my rifle from shoulder to shoulder and back to parade rest. Both officers strongly suggested that I get lost at the sports center the day of the inspection. I took their advice. Going to the Sport's Center was a good thing. Sgt. Frankie who was in charge of the center was a great guy. He made sure that I had access to everything in the center. His soft spoken manner did not match his huge frame. At one time he was one of Joe Louis' sparing partners. (Joe Louis was the Heavy Weight Boxing Champion of the World for a number of years).

During basic training, I became good friends with two guys: George Nelsen from Audubon and Bob Jones from Moorestown. These guys made basic training somewhat fun. Either, during Basic Training or shortly thereafter, we got together for dinner. Our first dinner, with our significant others, was at George's parent's home in Audubon. Our second dinner was at my mother's house in Palmyra. My mom's menu was steak with blue cheese topping, baked potato, and a salad, all of this and dessert in a candlelit setting. George's date was a girl from Palmyra that I knew. With six people for dinner, I hope I gave my mom some money for the food? Sometimes we take our parents for granted. Not a good thing.

After eight weeks of basic training, I was re-assigned to Fort Dix for the next eight weeks for advanced infantry training. The first or second day after reporting for assignment, I received a call to report to the staff sergeant in the office. He told me he was from Jamaica and recognized my name. He had been home on vacation when I competed in the Caribbean Games in Jamaica. Track and field was big in Jamaica and Sgt. Southerland was a fan. He made sure I did what was necessary in the morning before I was excused to train for the Olympics Trials in the afternoon. In church, I once heard the phrase, "somebody bigger than you and I is looking out for you." I certainly had somebody looking out for me, both in basic and advanced basic training.

After advanced basic training, I received orders for my permanent assignment at Fort Dix. It was like having a regular 8-to-5 job. My job was to assist the commanding officer with any task he needed done. My main job was to supply the troops with clothes and shoes.

Being in the Army is a commitment to serve your country. Fulfilling this commitment was full of joy. Housed in our barracks was Rosey Grier, on leave from the New York Giants football team, Sherman Plunkett, on leave from the Baltimore Colts and basketball players Wally Choice, Al Clinkscale, and Si Green, from the Cincinnati Royals. The basketball guys teamed up with former LaSalle College and Philadelphia Warriors great Tom Gola and others to form the Fort Dix basketball team. The Team had star power that dominated their competition. Pop Vernon, Basketball Guru from Riverside, New Jersey was present for all of their home games; he may have traveled to away games. As a Jersey guy, I rooted for Wally Choice from Montclair, New Jersey. Hanging around these guys made me feel small. All of them plus my roommate, Roy Goldbourne, were 6'4" tall or better.

Despite all of their success, the star athletes were regular guys. When I took them to my home in Palmyra, they didn't flaunt their celebrity. When we went to the driving range in Cinnaminson, some of us looked bad swinging that golf club. I think the lady on duty at the driving range had to laugh to herself. Being good in sports doesn't always transfer to the game of golf.

I knew Rosey Grier from our college days. He was on Penn State's track team and football team. When he came to the track meets, he brought his shot put, discus and singing voice. He was always singing in the locker room. My singing voice went silent when Rosey was on the scene. When his teammate and my chief competitor, Rod Perry from Coatesville, PA was present, I really went silent, he had a great voice too. He beat Harrison Dillard at the Philadelphia Inquirer Meet at Convention Hall when he was a freshman at Penn State. When I knew I had to run against him, I worried all week. Our shuttle hurdle team beat Penn State's shuttle hurdle team, anchored by Rod Perry at the Penn Relays. Later, I saw Rod in several television shows. Rosey and I were now teammates on the Fort Dix and First Army Track Team. On the plane to Fort Hood Texas, for the All Army Championships, Rosey told me he bought a new shirt but needed cuff links. I loaned him a pair of mine that was the last time I saw those cuff links. I thought a professional football player could afford a pair of cuff links?

Before I competed in the All-Army Championships, I was part of Fort Dix relay team that competed in the sprint medley relay at the Penn Relays. I was confident that our team would win. Our anchorman, Tom Courtney, would run the last leg. I knew Tom from our college days, when he was at Fordham. In our senior year of college, the two of us went to California and roomed together for the National Collegiate Championships. Tom won the half mile championship in California. At the Penn Relays, I knew if Tom was within 100 yards of the leader in the medley relay, he would catch whoever was ahead of him.

With two career soldiers in their thirties on the team, Tom was about 100 yards behind when he got the baton. As I knew he would, Tom made up the deficit and we won the race.

In the past, I had won several important races by inches. Tom saw those races and changed my training regimen. Tom had turned me into a certified crazy person. My regiment before I started training with Tom did not include any runs more than 330 yards. Tom, however, had me running distances of 660 yards. Not just once during a practice but several times. On occasions, he would make me run 880 yards. With his success, there was no reason to doubt him. My new training regimen served me well.

Tom was a member of the 1956 Olympic team. He went on to win the Olympic gold medal in the half mile race. Before that, we flew to Frankfurt, Germany, on our way to Berlin to compete in the International Military Track and Field Championships. The flight from New York to Frankfurt had a little drama. Half way across the Atlantic Ocean, the pilot informed the passengers that we have engine trouble. He told us that he was confident that we could make it to the Azores (an Island off Portugal). His next message, "put on your Mae West (Life Vest)". Tom said, "Charlie if they have to ditch the plane in the cold frigid

Atlantic Ocean, the Mae West won't keep us from freezing to death". Obliviously, we made it safely to the Azores and on to Frankfurt. In Frankfurt we met our other teammates. We stayed a couple of days in Frankfurt and Nuremberg to train before going to Berlin. While in Frankfurt and Nuremberg we did some sightseeing. We saw some remnants of World War II. Bullet holes were still visible on some of the buildings. After our training sessions, some guys said we were showering in the same places where people were gassed. It's hard to believe that the shower heads that provided water for us could have been the instruments of death, for others. Before our flight to Berlin, we had to report to a special building in Nuremberg (Palace of Justice) to get clearance from the Russian Government to fly over Russian airspace to get to Berlin. Each of us received a letter, written in Russian granting us clearance. I tried to save the letter although I couldn't read anything but my name, eventually the letter was lost.

At the time of departure we looked at the runway and saw a combat military type plane that would be the one to take us to Berlin. When we entered the plane we recognized that it wasn't a regular passenger aircraft. It had bucket seats, on each side of the plane, and a low ceiling. Before we took off, we were instructed to put on a parachute. The conversation after putting on the parachute was somewhat interesting. Our thinking, we have these parachutes in case the plane is fired upon. Some guys said they would jump out of the plane if we encountered trouble. Others said, no way were they going to jump. I don't remember what I said, probably nothing. When we arrived in Berlin, Germany was still divided into East and West Germany. I think the stadium, for the competition, was in East Berlin. I remember going through a gate to get to the stadium. The wall that separated

East and West Berlin was still up. There was a big difference in the two Berlins. West Berlin looked like a first class city. East Berlin looked like it belonged to another country. When we entered the stadium to train, some of us were overcome with emotion. Twenty years ago in this stadium, the legendary Jesse Owens had won four gold medals in the 1936 Olympics. Some of us remember hearing how Jesse Owens was treated by Hitler. Before our competition, we had a chance to see some parts of East Berlin. Two things stood out. We went to a museum, when we entered we saw a big Mosaic on the wall, of a face, most of us said, "Joe Louis". The other thing that impressed us, was visiting the training facilities of the East German athletes. Their trainer's room looked like a hospital. Everything we saw, dealing with training facilities was first class.

PHOTOGRAPHS PROVIDED COURTESY OF THE U. S. ARMY

All Army Track Team –Fort Hood Texas

PHOTOGRAPH PROVIDED COURTESY OF THE U. S. ARMY

All Army Track Team

PHOTOGRAPH PROVIDED COURTESY OF THE U. S. ARMY

Training Site- Formia, Italy

200 meter race in Berlin, Germany

Training Contingent at Formia, Italy

A little R & R in Berlin, Germany

Singing "My Ole Kentucky Home"

The American Contingent entertaining the Italian Sports Officials

Willi Williams and I taking in the sites in Naples, Italy

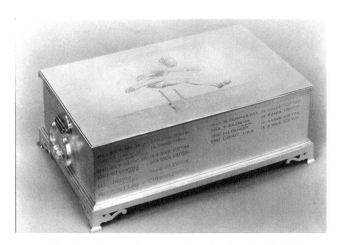

Replica of Trophy won - London England 1958

Don Bragg and Charlie Pratt

SURPRISE AWARD for 50 years' service was presented Dan Ferris, fourth from left, by A.A.U. past presidents at a luncheon in the Biltmore Hotel, Dayton, Ohio, June 22. Ferris was honored for his service with the A.A.U., including 30 years as secretary-treasurer. The inscription on the gold plaque bears the signatures of the eight living past presidents under whom Ferris has served, and the current president, Carl Hansen. L to r, Lou Wilke, Willard N. Greim, President Hansen, Mr. Ferris, James A. Rhodes, Albert F. Wheltle and Judge Jeremiah T. Mahoney.

The American team of Al Cantello, Tom Courtney, Tom Henderson, Earl Glaze, Ken Kave, Ira Muchinson, Bob Rittenberg, Willie Williams and I all performed very well. Ira Muchinson and Willie Williams both set the world record in the 100 meter dash in the competition. I won the 110 meters high hurdles and the 200 meter dash. Along with Ira, Willie and Ken Kave, I was part of the 4 x 100 relay team that won and gave me my third gold medal.

After the meet in Berlin, Ken Kave, Morgan State College, Bob Rittenberg, a good friend from Harvard University, (stayed at his parent's house a few days when we trained at Harvard). Willie Williams, National Collegiate Sprint Champion, University of Illinois and I traveled to Italy, to conduct clinics for the Italian Army Athletes. Ken Kave was the only Commissioned Officer in the group. When he was in uniform we had to salute him and address him as Lieutenant Kave. He really looked great and special, in his officer's uniform. Being an officer he couldn't stay in the same building with the rest of us.

The training site in Formia located halfway between Rome and Naples, was an excellent facility. The United States didn't have facilities like this for their athletes. Our living arrangements were very good, though we had to adjust our eating pattern. Our biggest meal was around noon time. In the evening, we had soup and a sandwich, plus a piece of fruit. The piece of fruit was on a plate with a knife. We realized that we were to cut the fruit instead of just picking it up with our hands and eating it.

International relations were put to a test when we tried to get the chef to make us a pizza. He didn't speak English and we didn't speak Italian. When he prepared the crust with just a bit of tomato sauce, we raised our voice and used our hands, hoping he would understand that we wanted some cheese and sausage on his creation. We settled for the chef's plain tomato pie.

Our first full day training on the track was an eye opener. The track was in excellent shape. They had a man whose job was to walk continuously around the track and fill in spike marks. During the week, we enjoyed demonstrating our training methods to the Italian officials and coaches. With our free time, we would visit the resort hotels bordering the Mediterranean Sea, a short distance across the highway from our training site. Some of the soldiers in the Italian Army would pick us up in a bus after dinner and show us some of the local sites in the mountains. One site in the mountains gave us a scare. Soldiers came in the Pub with machine guns. Our guest assured us that we were in no danger. Our group was crazy enough to go out again with our host after joking that we wouldn't put ourselves in jeopardy again.

Some of the best experiences of this trip were the time we spent in the cities of Naples, Rome, Sorrento and Pompeii. In those places, antiquity unfolded and came alive right before our eyes. When I saw the Coliseum in Rome and the ruins of Pompeii, I thought no way – how did people build those structures? While we were in Rome, we gave a clinic at the stadium where the 1960 Olympics would take place. A lady at the clinic told me that if you throw a penny in the famous fountain, as seen in the movie, "Three Coins in the Fountain," I would return for the 1960 Olympic Games. I found the fountain and threw my penny in. Well, it didn't work for me. Later I found out that you had to throw the penny a certain way over your shoulder. Guess I didn't throw the penny the right way.

The last night at the training site, a wonderful banquet was given for our group. The Italian group sang American songs in English. Thank heaven they gave us the words to the songs because we didn't know them. Example, "My Ole Kentucky Home."

After that European trip, we returned to our respective military bases. At this time, I had traveled to various countries in Europe and West Africa, plus Jamaica. Those trips were made possible because of Dan Ferris, secretary treasurer of the Amateur Athletic Union. Mr. Ferris was small in stature but big in his influence on amateur athletics. He was very good to me. Mr. Ferris sent me to Florida and back to Europe before I got out the Army.

My two years in the Army provided me with a lifetime of precious memories. From the enlisted men to the non-commissioned and commissioned officers, I couldn't have asked for more. The jam sessions in the barracks and locker rooms were special. We didn't need instruments. Voices like Rosey Grier and the availability of a foot locker or wooden bench was sufficient. If Al Cantello, Olympic javelin thrower, was in the mix, he played his harmonica. My buddies would only let me bang on a foot-locker or wooden bench. They said, "Why spoil a good thing with your voice."

When it was time for me to get out of the Army, I had mixed emotions. How would I adjust to civilian life? Fortunately, my first job was just across the street from the Army base. I still had access to my friends who were still stationed at Fort Dix. Don Bragg, a good friend from the base was a frequent visitor to my classroom. Hollywood wanted Don to be the future Tarzan. I don't know what happened, but people always liked hearing his Tarzan call and he liked doing it. I was always afraid he would do the Tarzan call in the classroom. Don and I trained together at the Bordentown Military Institute and Lawrenceville Prep School. Don went on to win the 1960 Olympic Pole Vault Championship. When his career was over he opened a summer camp for disadvantaged youth in the New Jersey Pines area. His camp stressed academics and physical activities. Josh Culbreath and I were there for the opening ceremonies. We stayed in touch until he moved to California. I was fortunate, some 20+ years after leaving the Army, to be reunited with Lt. Kenneth Conover while I was working at Rancocas Valley Regional High School.

Lt. Conover came to the guidance office to register his son for school. We talked about our time in the Army. I thanked him again for helping me during basic training. If it wasn't for it being an Olympic year, I might have considered a career in the Army.

Villages in the
WORKPLACE

More than once, I have heard athletes talk about life-learned lessons by participating in sports. These lessons can apply to our daily life as well as in one's workplace.

For example, sports teach that individual goals should be in concert with team goals. Sports can teach you to be mentally strong. That strength allows you to know, in your mind, that you are ready for the tasks that await you.

My daughter Jenni took horseback riding lessons at an early age. When it came time to ride her horse, I thought someone would bring it to her ready to ride. Wrong, she had to do everything herself, and she did. When she came out the stable pulling this big animal I was amazed. If someone asked me to do what Jennie did, I would have said, no thanks? Jenni looked and acted like she was around horses every day. I saw people around Jennie's generation who achieved because they believed they could.

Renee Chambers-Liciaga and Ron Chambers my other children are also mentally strong and feel that they are prepared for the task at hand. Renee trained to be a dancer and entertainer. When she auditioned for various shows, she was successful most of the time. "Why, because she displayed confidence in her craft". She knew what she wanted and didn't let barriers keep her from her goals.

Ron wanted to ride his motorcycle alone to California. He did it. "Why, because he was confident in his ability after careful planning". He wasn't burdened with doubts, and what ifs.

Being flexible is another lesson learned in sports. You may want to play a certain position, and the coach wants you to play another position on the team. You learn to adapt and be flexible to new opportunities. The same transition may occur when college students graduate and accept employment not related to their college major. One of my college friends, a philosophy major, started his career selling insurance and ended up as a successful stockbroker.

When Vern Dixon told me to seek a career in education, although different from my previous career plan, I had no problem with his advice. Dreams of a job in the business world disappeared.

When I came home from the competition, people in Palmyra planned activities to honor me. All of that was good, but I had other concerns. In a few weeks, my Army career would be over and I would need a job. The movers and shakers in Palmyra entertained the possibility of me being the first person of color to be a toll collector at the Tacony-Palmyra Bridge. No disrespect to toll collectors, but I didn't go to college to become a toll collector.

One businessman in the community suggested I seek a teaching position in the Palmyra school system. I spoke with one school administrator who encouraged me to get an application for employment. I was told I could teach school on an emergency teaching certificate. Enrollment in night school to gain full certification as a teacher would be mandatory.

I returned my application to the school's superintendent's

office (not Dr. John Geissinger). The businessman I talked to went to the Board of Education to see what action was taken on my application. To his surprise, the Board didn't know anything about my application. From the buzz I heard, Palmyra's school system was not ready for a black male on their faculty. I didn't panic because I was still in the Army. My discharge date was set for the last week in August

All was not lost; somehow Mr. John Mongon, superintendent of Burlington County Schools, knew I was looking for a job. He sent a message to me to come to his office in Mt. Holly. He had two jobs for me, one in Vincentown and the other in Pemberton. I took the sixth grade teaching position in Pemberton Township. I left his office with the information needed to get an emergency certificate to teach school.

The titles won in track had been great. But they didn't offer opportunities to earn a living. The title of teacher offered a chance to have a rewarding career.

When I started my career as a teacher, I had mixed feelings. Would the people in the school system be supportive and caring individuals? Would my lack of teacher training handicap me? My life style underwent a dramatic change. My career as a teacher had to be my top priority.

In my 37 year tenure as an educator, I had few major issues. However, like most people, I faced some bumps in the road.

When I went back to school to get my master's degree in student personnel services so that I could become a guidance counselor, I hit a bump. The professor for the first course, Introduction to Guidance, first night asked this question. "How many of you would consider becoming an administrator after spending time as a counselor?" I raised my hand and the professor had me stand up and identify myself. He told the class he questioned my sincerity in becoming a counselor. After class, unknown students came to me and suggested I transfer to another college, since this professor may make it difficult for me to complete the program. However, I stuck it out, although I got a "C" grade in both the mid-term and final grade. When I asked to see my test, I was denied the opportunity. In the second class with the same professor, I had the same results. One more "C" in any course and I would be dismissed from the program.

One incident in the second course, almost took all the wind out of my sails. I was asked a question on the homework. When I gave the right answer the professor told the class, Mr. Pratt did do his homework." I was embarrassed and fuming inside. When I got home I went to the bathroom and looked in the mirror and began to cry.

I asked myself, "Why is this happening to me"? My self-esteem all but disappeared. Along came a savior named Blossom Nissman, also in the program. She came to me and said, "The professor is not a bad person. He may be affected by the social chaos in our country". It was the time when riots were breaking out in some cities in the country. Since I looked like the few who were engaged. I guess I had to be a bad person. Blossom, told me she was planning a party at her home and the guest list would include several classmates and their families, the professor and his family, including my family. The party was a success; the professor's family embraced our family. A success not because our family gained acceptance. Success because it was clear that we shared similar family values and challenges such as good educational opportunities for our children, access to middle class life style and adequate housing. We had more in common than our differences. Before the party was over, I suspect the professor's wife put her stamp of approval on the Pratt family. When the lady, wife or mother put her stamp of approval on something, the rest of the family usually falls in line.

Blossom was true to what was preached in the first course of the guidance program. Counselors must be change agents. Blossom was truly a change agent – she changed the culture and thinking of many people in the program. She encouraged socialization and formed a study group.

Most students in the program, including me, reached their goal of receiving a Master's degree. With a lingering bitterness, I didn't participate in the graduation ceremony. Thanks to Blossom, in time, my bitterness faded away.

Blossom went on to work in various schools and administrative agencies in Burlington County. Her position required her to visit my school, Rancocas Valley Regional High School. She would always visit my office when she was in the building.

During one of her visits, she asked if she could bring a visitor on her next visit. I told her yes. Guess who she brought? The professor I had a problem with in the graduate program.

They came back several times to visit with me. The sight of seeing the professor did not conjure any hard feelings against him. I was doing what I wanted to do, surrounded by good people. I even went back to the college to speak to one of the classes in the guidance program. The bump in the road came several years into my teaching career. My relationships with people helped me to deal with adversity. My background in sports also played an important role. Once I was in a race I always finished, never quit. In the indoor IC4A Championships my sophomore year, I pulled a leg muscle in the semifinal race, but still qualified for the final race. I had to run the final race injured to get the points for the team (I jogged not ran the race).

My career in education covered three school districts; Pemberton township, Riverside and Rancocas Valley Regional High School, all located in Burlington County. My first 10 years as a teacher, I also worked part-time as a toll collector at the Tacony-Palmyra Bridge. I also worked with the maintenance staff at Pemberton Township during the Christmas and Easter holidays, cleaning classrooms and floors.

When I lost my summer job temporarily at the bridge, I cut grass to earn money. Later in August, I regained my summer job back at the bridge. However, I continued to cut grass for four or five more years. The work ethic I learned as a young person, I did what I had to do.

My decision to seek a career in education was one of the best decisions I made. The staff at the three districts were both good educators and good people. They created a good work environment.

One of the true blessings in my career at Rancocas Valley Regional High School (R.V.) came from a lady named Evelyn Horner. This lady had the responsibility of cleaning the guidance office. When she came to my office, she made a fuss over me and my office. I let her know how much I appreciated the attention she gave me. When she passed, her daughter found a letter from her mother requesting that I attend her funeral and serve as a pallbearer. Mrs. Horner's request was honored. She was a special person.

My path to Rancocas Valley Regional High School came through Bill Gordon and Dick Hoffman, both I met at a counselor's conference. They convinced me that R.V. needed someone that didn't look like them. Amen to that. After hearing about some unrest among the minority students at R.V., I told Gordon and Hoffman I would give it some thought. The two of them arranged for me to meet the school superintendent, Mr. Fred Evans.

Prior to meeting Mr. Evans, several black students met with him. They wanted to interview me before he made a decision. They wanted to know if I was "black enough." Did they think I was a white man, masquerading in black face?

Mr. Evans asked them, "Did you interview your English teacher, your math teacher or your social studies teacher?" They said no. His reply: "Then you won't interview Mr. Pratt, either."

After I got the job, some students continued to have a problem with me. I made it clear to the minority students that I was not their "brother" or "bro" or "homey": My name is Mr. Pratt.

Some black students thought I was hired for them to have somebody to rap with. I told those students I have a job just like the other counselors. When you come to my office, come prepared to talk about your education. Don't use my office visit as an excuse because you don't want to go to class. Mr. Evans always supported my desire to be a counselor to all students assigned to me. I didn't want to be known as the "black counselor" for the black students, although the black students had access to me.

I knew how good the sports program was at R.V. long before I joined the staff, I coached both cross country and track at Pemberton and Riverside. My teams never beat R.V.'s teams. The old adage, if you can't beat them, join them – that's what I did.

During my tenure at R.V., I worked with two athletic directors, Ray Hoagland and Carmen Cella. Both were successful coaches; both brought a commitment to their position that earned them respect from the staff and students. Under their leadership, the sports program was a compliment to the school's academic program. Ray and Carmen and their coaches worked with teachers and counselors to help student athletes succeed in high school. They also helped the athletes take the next step after high school. A good number went on to great careers beyond sports. Some continued their sports career in college. Fans of professional football may know that Franco Harris, Irving Fryar and Alonzo Spellman are graduates of Rancocas Valley Regional High School. I enjoy telling people Irving Fryar and I were in high school together.

R.V. was a great example of a good work environment. Very few employees left R.V. because of poor working conditions, a great testimony to the entire staff.

Within the large village of the school were the small villages, better known as the academic disciplines or departments. Of course, the guidance department was my favorite village. A member of the department for 23 years, I enjoyed coming to work.

It started with Dr. Tyler Hess, our director. He was organized, with written job assignments for each month along with written job descriptions. He put together a school profile that included information on the regional districts. The profile was a requirement for institutions of higher education. It was available to parents and others seeking information about the school.

Dr. Hess' staff were on board with him, starting with Jane Brooks, secretary, and her assistant Laura Pagenkoph, and the following counselors: Bill Gordon, Dick Hoffman, Marcia Miner, Bill Trefz and me, Charles Pratt. This group created a great working atmosphere. We were truly a family who cared about each other. Though we all had very different personalities, it worked for us. It also worked for our students.

After a few years, I replaced Dr. Hess when he moved to the school's Child Study Team. My new assignment included the supervision of the following departments; the Child Study Team, the guidance office, the nurses and the special education department.

In addition, I worked closely with Mrs. Liz Anderson on the scheduling program and Mrs. Sandra Symczk with the home instruction program. Charlene Jennings and Raj Makara were a great help to me with the special education program. All of these folks made my job easy.

In time there were some personnel changes in the guidance department. Marcia Miner left the department to enter private practice. Laura Pagenkoph left the department for another position in the school. She was replaced by Linda Morrell, who, in time, became a teacher and counselor. She was replaced by Linda Adams.

To fill counselor vacancies, the following people were members of the guidance department for an extended period of time: Donna Aromando, Barbara Hannmann, John Mockus, Marie Phillips and Roy Ridgway.

The key to any office, I found, is the person who is the first contact for those who enter the office. That person for our office was Jane Brooks. She greeted everyone in a professional manner. She was the heart and soul of our department. She helped to create a family atmosphere in the guidance office.

Note about counselors Bill Gordon, Dick Hoffman, Roy Ridgway, and Bill Trefz. All were coaches at some point in their career. Many athletes give credit to their coaches for teaching them about life skills as well as sports. I have learned about life skills from my colleagues, especially Bill Gordon.

Other than the guidance people, there were other contributing factors that made it easy for me to go to work every day. Henry Huss, the principal for most of my tenure at R.V., had a special leadership quality. He didn't try to over manage the staff or the various departments. He, along with his assistants, Dr. Joe Beringer and Joel Poplar, treated the staff as professionals and trusted their commitment. He was open to suggestions. The trust Henry Huss, placed in the teaching staff, had far reaching benefits. Student and staff unrest was at a minimum. Students often mirror the demeanor of their teachers.

This may be a poor analogy, but you have to take chances sometime. The teaching staff, in any school is the core of the educational program, like mom, in the home. If momma ain't happy, nobody is happy. I think Henry Huss, Joel Poplar and Dr. Joe Beringer tried to make momma happy without compromising their integrity. When my colleagues recommended me to be their supervisor, Henry Huss accepted their recommendation.

A few stories about other colleagues:

- Carol Graf, an English teacher, received a number of awards for being an outstanding educator. I asked her if she would erase her name on one of those certificates and put my name on it. I had the Wite-Out ready. She wouldn't do it.

- I once gave Trudy Menne, supervisor of the liberal arts department, a two page letter to proof read. When I got the letter back, I didn't recognize it. Attached to the letter was a note, "Charles: is English your second language?" I didn't feel bad.

- Val Best's (secretary in the main office) family invited me to their home for breakfast. She wouldn't let me in the house.

- June Dreger, a teacher in the reading program – nobody is that nice.

If I overstate the goodness of working at R.V. I have several reasons. On the outside I've heard people lament their poor working conditions. That includes the people they work with. Others can't wait to retire. Some of those conditions probably existed at R.V. but it didn't define the culture at R.V. People who cared about their colleagues is what I witnessed at R.V. Socialization outside of school crossed department boundaries. Further proof that R.V was a close knit group, is the number of retirement groups that meet frequently. Traveling together is another activity shared by retirees. Some groups are open to spouses and friends.

Members of the guidance department met regularly until illness and death took its toll on the group. Henry Huss, his wife Henrietta, Joel Poplar's wife Lynn, Dr. Joe Beringer, Dave Fletcher, his wife Pat, Trudy Menne and I continue to have what we call cabinet meetings at various eateries in Burlington County. Dave Fletcher is the only one who gets out of control. Can't imagine how he would act if he drank anything other than ice tea.

I also participate in a men's breakfast group that is very special. To be part of this group, you must be able to laugh at the simplest thing. When men come together twice a month, it shows how much they care about each other. Rocky DiGiacomo and Glen Wolfrom (a high school math teacher and a high school science chairperson, respectively) are responsible for the success of the breakfast group. Rocky will call guys if they miss a few meetings. Some guys who left R.V to work in other districts rejoined the guys now at breakfast. The men's breakfast group meets the second and fourth Mondays of every month at the Esquire Diner at Route 206 and Route 537, outside of Mt. Holly.

When I see Bill Hosback, John Osworth and Tony Petrillo, I'm reminded how these guys helped me put in a patio at my house. When I offered them money, Tony looked at me like I was crazy. Later Tony and John put in my attic fan. Seeing Dick Randolph also reminded me of the advice he gave me when I was thinking about retirement. As a veteran, he said, "If I worked one more year passed my target date my pension would get a little boost". When I went to the pension office they confirmed the advice given to me Dick Randolph.

The Men's Breakfast Group

Ed Adams	Ron George	John Osworth
Roy Ridgway	Dave Bell	Nate Herreshoff
Tony Pertillo	Jack Riley	Dr. Joe Beringer
Ray Hoagland	Vince Phillips	Lynn Schoepske
Roger Budd	Bill Hosbach	Bob Poole
Wayne Smith	Bud Ceremsak	Jim Matarese
Joel Popler	John Stanley	John Demby
Mike Morse	Dave Powell	Don Wisniewki
Dave Fletcher	Stu Murray	Charlie Pratt
Glenn Wolfrom	Harry George	Dick Randolph
Tom Wurtenburger		

Belonging to these R.V. retirement groups has been good for my mental health.

Retirement can be a big challenge for some people. The cost of breakfast with good people is relatively cheap.

Rancocas Valley Regional High School was the last stop on

my career journey. However, I still have fond memories of stops at Pemberton and Riverside school districts. I still share a friendship with John Sapanaro from our Pemberton days. The same can be said about Bill Tyler until his passing several years ago. Bill and I were together at least once a month for 50 years. Ken Ellis a colleague at Pemberton and I spent years of quality time together.

Each of the three districts provided a different experience. At Pemberton where I started my career, my focus was on trying to be a competent teacher. There was some social interaction but low on the priority list.

After seven years at Pemberton, I moved over to Riverside. The Riverside High School staff, like me, was a little older and confident in our role as educators. The guys at Riverside had an excess amount of energy and wanted to have fun. And fun we had.

In my nine years at Riverside, we enjoyed dinner before going to Phillies night games, ice skating, cookouts, house parties, softball games, socials after basketball games (at Joe and V. France's house and Jesse Welsh's house), Sunday morning basketball games, boating (thanks to Mr. K.) and the infamous fall and spring frolic at Dora's.

Dora had a farm house off the Rancocas Creek in Delanco. She and her family catered parties at her home. The dessert, homemade ice cream and apple pie, was always a hit. The dinner was just the prelude to the real action: two poker games, one for high rollers and the other for the amateurs like me. When I inquired about the bathroom Ron Frey, pointed to the door and told me to keep walking, you'll find it I found it alright. It was a big bathroom. Some people call it the Rancocas Creek. I guess it was my initiation into the Brotherhood of Fun.

When the weather turned cold, someone suggested that we go ice fishing. "Great idea", I said, though I had no idea how to do so. No one in my neighborhood ever went ice fishing. When I showed up on the appointed day, I was dressed for the occasion. I thought my choice of beverage, hot chocolate, was appropriate for the weather condition. The group let me know the proper drink for this outing was ice cold beer. Did we catch any fish? I don't think so. Who cares, we had fun.

I remember two parties we had in our home in Moorestown for this Riverside group. One was a cookout. Joe France came to the backyard wheeling a new wheel barrow. At first, I thought it was a gift for the house. No –he and his wife Vi filled the wheelbarrow with soda and fruit. My children still talk about how beautiful the wheelbarrow looked.

With all the great activities I shared with the Riverside group, there was one that brought me down to earth. Elaine and Russ Paul were hosts to many socials at their home on a beautiful lake. At one of their outings, their community had a canoe festival. Our host thought it would be good to take my two young children and me on a canoe ride. During the ride, we passed one of the floats in the festival that drew our attention. The float had several people wearing white hoods over their heads. I'm not sure their dress included sheets. But, I am sure the float had a replica of a Black man being hanged. How do you explain that to your young children? Our host expressed his feelings of disappointment and shame to the offending float. I told my children that people can live in an environment and not be a part of the environment

I learned from the Riverside group you can enjoy yourself without sacrificing your commitment to your career. These guys took their jobs seriously but not themselves. They taught me that the key to enjoying longevity in the workplace might be finding that proper balance between work and leisure activities. Any attempt to name all the people I worked with and the good residents of Riverside will only end in failure. The following people however, I still share a relationship; the circus ringmaster, Ron Frey, Harry Johnstone, Bernie Smith and Charlie Olgiata. Until their passing, I stayed in touch with Rocky Cancellieri, Joe France, Doug Frambes, Joe Maratea and Pop Vernon.

The period between age 50 and 60 was a good time. My colleagues appeared comfortable with who they were. Working and social relationships only got stronger. At times, I was engaged with other seniors in conversations regarding longevity. Most of us realized that we escaped some of the pitfalls others had experienced on their jobs or in their life. We were fairly secure in thinking retirement was on the horizon.

Before I knew it, age 60 was looking me in the face. My retirement papers were being prepared. It's hard to describe that last day of employment. I could only think sometimes the journey is more important than the destination. I enjoyed the ride.

My journey took thirty six years. It ended when my staff had a limousine pick up my secretary, Jane Brooks (who also retired) and me at the school. It was a short ride to Robin's Nest, a local eatery. Oh, what a ride it was, only to be greeted by members of the Child Study Team, guidance, nurses and special education departments. The group showed their appreciation for our work and our relationship.

It ain't over 'til it's over. I don't know where this phrase came from, but it defined me. Five years after I retired, I went back to work in my old guidance department, due to a last-minute opening, after a counselor left for a job closer to his home.

The first day of work, on a Thursday, I had second thoughts when I was told that a family new to the school wanted a conference with me on Monday. They were concerned about their high-ranking child who was in his senior year. I was advised the family already talked with several members in the guidance department. After hearing that information, my weekend was a disaster. I wasn't ready for a parent conference this soon!

I decided the best approach is the simplest one: be honest with the family during the conference. I told the parents about my background and told them that I could deliver anything their child may need but not with the use of a computer. The conference went very well. The student came to see me almost every day, sometimes more than once a day. The parents stayed in constant contact with me.

During the eight months I spent back in the department, I received all the help I needed from the guidance staff, especially with the new technology available. Joel Poplar and Dr. Joe Beringer were available with problems beyond the scope of guidance. Claudia Gifford was also a help to me. Marie Phillips, supervisor of the guidance department, knew that I struggled with the new technology and was available for helped. Counselors

Donna Armando, Paula Johnson, Leah Ream, George Corcoran and John Mockus made my return to R.V. a rewarding experience. I wasn't too proud to ask them for help when my computer didn't obey me.

Returning to work after five years wasn't an easy task. However, that family I had a conference with when I first came back to work validated my efforts. Their child was later accepted to the Ivy League university of their choice. Several weeks before his high school graduation, his parents came to see me. The mother said, "Mr. Pratt, the Lord brought you back to R.V. to help my child."

I left R.V. for the last time, knowing that I had done what any athlete hopes to do: hit a homerun, make a touchdown, sink the winning basket, beat Milt Campbell in the hurdles. At least that's how I felt after that mother's comments to me that day.

One of many retirement celebration's

Rancocas Valley High School Senior Night Diner
Left to right: Bill Gordon, Joe Holland, Carol Graf, Charlie Pratt, Liz
Braun, Claudia Gifford, Trudy Menne, Seated John Tettis

My Neighborhood

a Great Village

When I started looking for a home in the early part of 1980, I remember passing a new development in Marlton. I decided to stop at the sales office for this development. To my surprise, one of the sales consultants was a former student named Nancy Rice. After several visits looking at the sample homes, I was sold on a house.

After talks with Nancy and other sales associates, the deal to buy a house was complete. Several days after signing on the dotted line, I had flashbacks of a conversation I had with a friend in the 60'S. We had competed against each other in football and track in high school. Both of us were educators working in different school districts. We would meet at his relative's house and carpool together to take post-graduate courses. No doubt, this guy liked and admired me. He wanted me to leave my school and join him at his school. However, one night on our way home from class, he said," Charlie, I wouldn't want you living next to me. You would drive the value of my house down."

I don't know what precipitated that conversation, but I tried to ignore it. I believe if I had lived next to my friend, his house might increase in value.

Leaving the fifties and sixties and my friend's thinking behind, final preparations were made to move to Marlton. In March 1980, we moved to Thornwood Drive. A lot of thought was given to this move. Will a family of color come face to face with neighbors and a neighborhood who share the same views that my friend shared? Before moving in, I visited the house at different times of the day and walked around the property so I would be seen. Thankfully, we moved in and had no problems. The new house needed some work on the yard. Yard work gave me additional exposure in the neighborhood.

Some people create problems for themselves. I was one of those people. I would wave to my neighbor when he returned home from work. He would not acknowledge my wave. This continued for several weeks. While working in the backyard, a little boy four years old would come over and watch me work. The young boy, named David, was the son of the neighbor in question. Through him, I met his mother, Rose Mosca. Shortly after meeting Rose, she gave me some insight about the family. They had moved from northeast Philadelphia, where her husband Lou owned an Italian bakery. He was up early in the morning and when he had finished work, I think he just put his car on automatic pilot. He wasn't ignoring me; he had to concentrate on trying to get home safely. That concentration didn't stop until he was in his driveway.

Soon after, I met Lou. We talked frequently and in time we became more than neighbors; we became friends. He still ignores me on occasions in his car. David continued to visit me when I was in the backyard. From age four, if his parents were cooking outside and I was outside David made sure I got what they were cooking. David started cooking after he reached age 12 or 13. Rose and Lou did a good job raising their son. Sometimes teenagers forget about older folks. David never changed.

After high school, David went away to college. When he came home to see his parents, nothing really changed about him except at age four he only came up to my waist. Now I look up to him, in more than one way. The sweet innocence of youth I found in David as a young boy, I now see in a young man. Rose, Lou and David were truly gems as neighbors.

In the neighborhood, I met two of Rose and Lou's friends, Faye and Tom DeGaetano. Their home was four or five houses from ours. My first impression of Faye a sweet lady. I still can't find words to describe Tom. Tom was a car salesman. He and his brother Donny also had a nightclub act. They performed all over and on occasion the opening act for many well-known performers and bands. To know Tommy is to know someone who is always on stage. A simple greeting is all Tommy needs, to go into his nightclub act. Lou calls him the poor man's Seinfeld.

Tommy and I were partners in the neighborhood watch program. For two hours once a week in the evening, we would ride around the neighborhood – the best two hour live show of the week. When I visited Tommy and Faye at their home, I saw pictures of Tommy and his brother with well-known entertainers. Tommy also showed me films of their nightclub act.

As a salesperson selling high-end cars, Tommy always dressed like he was going to a fashion show. Every strand of hair was in place. He still thinks he's all that and a bag of chips (ask someone in Palmyra what that phrase means).

During the Christmas holidays, Sandra and I would join Faye and Tommy at the Mosca's house. It was a joy to hear the Moscas and DeGaetanos relive their long friendship and vacations together. Tommy would entertain us with one story after another. Rose and Faye would tell the stories that Lou and Tommy would omit on purpose – the embarrassing ones. My favorite story, told by Tommy. He parked his car in front of my dad's house in Palmyra. My dad's house was less than 100 yards from Kerbeck Enterprises. My dad had raked leaves in a pile near the curb. Tommy parked his car over the leaves. As he was walking to work, at Kerbeck his co-workers told him that his car was on fire. Something under the car had set the leaves on fire. His co-workers quickly put the fire out. Who did he think he was, parking his car in front of my dad's house? A good thing I didn't know him then. We were careful who we let on our street and in our neighborhood. What Tommy didn't know, people in Palmyra grew up with style. One day I told him the neighborhood wasn't big enough for both of us. Somebody had to go, and it wasn't going to be me.

In time, Tommy and Faye moved to a retirement community in Mt. Laurel. After Tommy and Faye moved, Rose considered the same move. When I told Sandra of Rose's intentions of moving, she was really upset. After a few tears, she said, "they can't leave because they are like family." Lou didn't want to move, thank heaven, and he won the battle. He would kid Rose and tell her she could go without him – but she joked that he wouldn't have anyone to cook for him. He said: "Don't worry … Charlie will cook." I would joke that my spaghetti sauce was better than his spaghetti gravy (an old family secret, from my distant cousin, Jim Materese).

Several years ago, we lost Rose. Her passing affected us like a close member of the family. She was a special lady. She would tell her friends how special Sandra and I were to her family. When she first got sick, she sent for Sandra to pray for her. Sometimes she would spend time in their enclosed patio. She would watch me work in the backyard. Sometimes, she would wave for me to come over to get something to eat. When I work in the yard, I really didn't want to stop. When it came to Rose, it was a joy to stop. Before her passing, sometimes Rose would fall usually at night. Lou spoke to me about those falls, he said, "If it happened again he might need help getting her up". He knew all he had to do is call. Late one night Lou called needing help, Rose had fallen again. When I went over I saw the position she was in, it would be difficult for both of us to position ourselves to help Rose. With a bad back and Lou's health situation, I was afraid that we might do more harm than good. Our daughter Renee and her husband, Peter Liciaga and children were staying with us, waiting to move into a house they bought. As a personal trainer, and Karate instructor Peter was in great shape. I asked Lou if I could get my son in law to help us. He agreed. I went back to the house, woke Peter up, and told him that we needed his help next door. Peter looked at the situation; he asked, "Where can I grab Rose without hurting her". Lou told Peter the best way to lift Rose. He then lowered his body, positioned his arms and picked her up and put her in a wheelchair. We all looked in amazement because Peter did something that used to take both Lou and I to do. Rose couldn't talk, but the look in her eyes, acknowledged what Peter had done for her. I mentioned this story for two reasons, first Peter not only helped Rose, he also saved both Lou and me from hurting ourselves. Second reason, in church the pastor will sometimes say "the Lord always has a Ram in the bush (if somebody can't do it he has somebody who can.)" Peter was the Ram, shortly after that incident, sons, David and Don came home, to help with their mother's care.

David, Rose and Lou Mosca

Stauffer Family, Conrad, Linda, Beth Anne, Julie and John Mark

In the past couple of years, Lou, Tommy and I get together for breakfast, lunch or trips to the shore. For 30 years, Sandra and I feel blessed to have had Lou and his family as neighbors. We still have the keys to their house. Lou lives by himself, we and the neighbors across the street keep an eye on him. One time we had to call the cops because we couldn't contact him. All was well.

If I ever had any doubts about the neighborhood, they soon disappeared after another incident years ago. I was trying to remove a tree in the front yard. A young man about eight years old named John Mark Stauffer walked by and saw I had a problem. He said, "Mister, don't try to move that tree by yourself. I'll go home and get my father and our small tractor and trailer and pull the tree out the hole." He went home and came back with his father, Conrad, and their equipment. The father pulled the tree out and hauled it away. When I tried to thank them, the young boy said, "We are here to serve." That phrase, "We are here to serve," took all the wind out of any lingering doubts I might have harbored about the neighborhood.

This Christian family, the Stauffers, served me and the community for a number of years. John Mark has continued to help me since the first meeting. Now 19, he and his family taught me something about serving the community. This young man started his own property maintenance business several years ago. With his work ethic and family support, the sky is the limit for John Mark.

Our other next-door neighbors are Peg and Jim Purdy. Jim and I talk about sports, our yards and flowers. We also share equipment used in the house or yard. Jim will always help you complete your project. Once he helped me shovel snow when we both had bad backs. When I tried to stop him, he told me that we were neighbors and that is what neighbors should do – help each other. Since Jim is built like a linebacker, he got no argument from me. Jim is a diehard Eagles fan. When they lose, he is not a happy camper.

We talk frequently with Peg and Mike Worchol, our neighbors cross the street, because they spent a lot of time in the front yard; especially Mike, who takes great pride in his yard. I really like both Jim and Mike because they are crazy like me when it comes to the yard. Their wives blame me for their husbands working in the yard all the time.

Peg Purdy can't really have a problem with me, because she always greets me with a friendly smile and a big, "Hi Chuck." Once or twice, I asked to borrow some spices from Peg Purdy. She would give me the whole container.

Growing up, neighbors often borrowed a cup of sugar, flour or some butter from each other. I brought that tradition to my next door neighbors. Once, when I was working in my yard on a hot day, I went in the house to get something to eat. When I looked for my can of Root Beer Lite, I had none. Knock, knock, Lou, I said, I need a can of Root Beer Lite to go with my lunch. Sure Chuck, he said, I think I can help you.

Now Peg across the street always greets me with a big hello, but I have to scold her on occasions when she fusses with Mike in the yard. I tell her to leave Mike alone. She wants to take Mike's job away in the yard. Some ladies just like to get their hands and feet dirty. Sandra, can't you see how much fun Peg has in the yard? Peg won't tell Sandra it's alright for ladies to get their hands dirty. My daughter Renee likes to work in the yard, but failed to convince Mom. Oh, I forgot – Mom grew up on Sixth Street in Palmyra.

To read more about my memories of my other neighbors and their families, please go to the appendix at the end of the book.

My Church

as a Village

Train a child in the way he should go and when he is old, he will not turn from it." Proverbs 22:6.

When I went to church as a young boy, I went to St. Paul Union American Methodist Episcopal Church in Palmyra. I don't remember going on a regular basis. When I was 11 or 12, I spent time on Saturdays and Sunday caddying at the Riverton Country Club instead of church. Did that mean I was devoid of religious training? I think not. The few times I went to church, I believe the pastor seized the moment to talk about the Lord and value of going to church.

When I was in eighth grade, I was one of the smallest kids in the class. I didn't go to my parents; I got down on my knees and prayed to the Lord to help me gain weight and grow taller. I probably turned to the Lord because I had written to Charles Atlas, a famous bodybuilder. The materials he sent me didn't work and caused my dad some embarrassment, since my mother thought he requested them. I had to admit it was me who sent for them. I threw the materials away. But I continued to pray. Within the next two years, I grew a little and had some minor success in sports – enough for me to think my prayers were answered.

During my high school years, our peer group went to Sunday night church services at a little church on 5th Street in Palmyra. We went there because it was something new and we had nothing else to do. That church later became the home for the Southerland family. Our group, Snookie Banks, Eddie Grimes and Billy King, also went to Jacob's Chapel in Mount Laurel on Sunday evenings. Jacob's Chapel was our choice when we heard that they had some young ladies going there. (Many years after high school, I revisited Jacob's Chapel, not because of the Pastor but to see his wife, my first cousin, Toylene Person and her sister Penelope Berringer). Some Baptist churches had Sunday evening services for young people. We went to some of those services as well, which gave us something to do on Sunday night.

Our motives to attend Sunday evening services were not always pure. However, sometimes the right environment cancels out the wrong motives. Again, I feel strongly that in each of those churches, when the pastor saw young people, something was said for us to carry away in our spiritual bank. During my college years there were times I went to St. John's Baptist Church in Scotch Plains with my father and Aunt Ethel Syers. On occasion, I would go with Lou Jones to his church, St. Catherine A.M.E. Zion Church, in New Rochelle, New York.

I knew that in my freshman year of college, I had spent many Sundays alone on the campus. When my grandniece, Laliah Pratt, decided to go to college in Connecticut, I talked with Rev. Joseph Bash, pastor of St. Paul UAME Church in nearby New Haven, Connecticut, and asked him to look out for her. I was told that Sister Delores Roy from our home church had already made contact with Sister Jackie Bracey from St. Paul, New Haven on behalf of my grandniece. Laliah told me that Sister Bracey and the folks at St. Paul have been a blessing to her. Laliah graduated from college in the spring of 2011.

Another college student from our church, Loren Dobbs, goes to Kean College in North Jersey. She has Rev. Adolphus Scott and their congregation at Trinity UAME Church in Newark available to her.

When I look back on my freshman year in college, I wish I had made a connection with a church in New York. It would have made my life easier. For the young people who go away for higher education, get help in finding a church with similar values as your home church. If you don't go to church or other place of worship, consider finding one.

In 1973-1974, my private life began to fall apart – I experienced marriage difficulties and my wife and I separated, then divorced. Thanks to my dad, my brother Merrill and his wife Katherine who opened their home to me. Their daughter, Kathy Merle, became my mother hen. She really took care of me. She continues to contribute to the health and welfare of all the family members connected to the Pratt and Cephas clan. Kathy reminds me of one of my aunts, but I don't remember which one (actually I do, but Kathy will spank me if I mention it … Aunt Ethel).

Despite all the support from family and friends, there was still something missing. That something was a connection to a church. After years of feeling a degree of success, I felt the pain of failure.

I wasn't sure I could swallow my pride to walk through the doors of St. Paul UAME Church in Palmyra with my chin up. However, what I learned in sports helped me walk through those doors. As a hurdler, I had to run over ten hurdles. In one National Championship, I hit the last hurdle and fell but I still got up and finished third in the race. Life sometimes is like a series of hurdles … sometimes you hit one, but you have to keep going.

When I hit one of life's hurdles, I didn't look around for someone to blame. It was my fault. I had to keep going.

Like most athletes, when you want to get better, you go to someone or a group of people who can help you. Some of those people could be found on Sunday morning in St. Paul UAME Church.

Within a few weeks of going, I felt comfortable returning to St. Paul. I did feel uncomfortable with one sermon I thought was directed at me (Sermon topic: "Sometimes People Wonder Why Things Happen to Them"). If it wasn't directed at me, why did people keep turning around to look at me? That's what I got for sitting in the back row. Now I sit near the first row in church.

Shortly after I returned to St. Paul, I felt like I was a member of the St. Paul family. After all, I was still the guy who had been christened at St. Paul as a kid. I was still the kid who stood up to deliver his Easter recitation, looked at the congregation, ran out the church and didn't stop until I got home. I never criticize a young person who has trouble speaking to an audience.

Two things were instrumental in the first two years that glued me to St. Paul. Not to take anything away from the pastors that served St. Paul, but I had a special bond with Rev. Dr. Milton Brooks. We talked about me being "a project in the making." I am still a project in the making.

The second was the formation of a male chorus. Thanks to Louise Vaughn and Lillian Cherry, who had the idea originally. Earlier I had joined the senior choir, after the passing of Uncle Moral Person.

Nothing against the senior choir, but when the men came together in fellowship, it was something special. Our fellowship flourished because of our leader and pianist, Lillian Cherry. Many of our rehearsals were at her house. Her home came alive with love and appreciation for each other. This wonderful lady didn't have much to work with so we tried to shower her with love as a substitute for our lack of talent. I think it worked, because she was a joy to work with.

We loved her so much that we didn't want any of her leftover food from dinner to spoil so we ate it. Leftover fish or chicken didn't have a chance. Her budget must have taken hit from the candy and cookie bills. We raided those jars. The guys couldn't wait to come back to Lillian's house each week for rehearsal.

The group included my dad, Charles M. Pratt, Gabe Austin, Lloyd Scott, Keith Austin, Gabe's son and me. The following men were part of the group for special programs, or for a limited period of time: Mickey Burroughs, Sister Cherry's sons, Derrick and George Jr., Wayne Carthorne, Merrill Pratt, Jr. (my nephew) and Ronald Stewart. In time, the chorus added three new permanent members: William Roy, Ossie Lecky and a member of the Scott family. For some reason, I can't remember his name.

After Lillian moved to the Midwest to be with her daughter, the male chorus was blessed with another great pianist, Yvonne Long. We never missed a beat in the transition of musicians. Sister Long has a nice way about her and is a joy to work with.

She may not feel that way about us. Maybe I shouldn't say us, because of one person. This person is one of the newer members.

When he came to choir rehearsal, with his music in a brown paper bag, I knew our rehearsals would never be the same again. I continue to forget his name but I recognize him when I see him. The only reason we keep him, is his so-so voice. In reality, with Sister Long's musical talent and the guy with the so-so voice, our chorus has raised the level of our performances. Mr. So-So's personality also has raised the level of our fellowship during rehearsal.

Every member of the group makes some kind of contribution at the rehearsals. With the comfort level we share, the men feel free to express themselves. In doing so, it's easy to see that we have grown spiritually. There was a time when I asked someone to give the opening or closing prayer they would look at me like I was crazy. Now you might have to get a ticket to get a turn to lead the prayer.

Several years ago, the men's choir of St. Paul joined forces with men from four other churches and formed a community choir. The following churches and men make up the community choir

- From Evergreen Baptist Church in Palmyra, Theodore Scott (I try not to say his name);

- James Butler and Donald Johnson represent St. Paul Baptist Church in Cinnaminson

- Our director and pianist Brother Carl Davis, Cordell Washington, Edward White and Melvin Williams are from Mt. Zion AME Church in Riverton

- John Jones from Woodcrest United Church of Christ, Philadelphia

When I thought the fellowship and joy exhibited by the men's choir of St. Paul was at the highest level, I was wrong. The community choir took fellowship, commitment and joy to a higher level.

Our goal was two-fold: to seek harmony in both our voices and fellowship to further serve the Lord through our music. Thanks to Brother Davis and the men, we stay true to our mission. Our rehearsals are filled with joy, praise and sometimes tears. Brother Davis has put together a great library of songs suitable for male voices.

When Brother Edward White gives the closing prayer following our closing songs, you know you have been blessed. When Theodore from Evergreen Baptist Church takes the lead and sings, "I am so Satisfied," get prepared to share the Kleenex box. Tears are sure to follow. Theodore is the fellow with the so-so voice. On a scale of 1 to 10, he deserves a 10+.

My life has been blessed by many villages. St. Paul has given me a chance to be a member of a village that blesses people.

St. Paul has always been known as that friendly welcoming and caring church. That positive identity was well-earned, not a shallow gift to make the people of St. Paul feel good about themselves.

Rev. Brooks had a lot to do with St. Paul's identity. Many people viewed Rev. Brooks and St. Paul as one. After he retired, Rev. Charles Anderson arrived. It became clear, after witnessing Rev. Anderson in homes, hospital visits and other situations around the community, that Rev. Anderson was approachable and dependable.

Despite additional commitments, Rev. Anderson added another one. He wanted to make Rev. Brooks' dream of building a new church a reality. The dream was also shared by the long standing members of St. Paul.

Rev. Anderson, above all, made the dream of a new church a reality. With the support of the congregation, Rev. Anderson and the building committee (Lorraine Austin, William Roy, Lloyd Scott and I), came together to start the building process. When Rev. Milton Brooks, who moved to Virginia, returned to the area; what a day it was seeing him walk through the doors of the new church. He preached just one Sunday in the new church. Rev. Brooks soon passed away, a short time before his 100th birthday.

As expected, the new church draws a lot of attention. It probably contributed to the increase for Rev. Anderson's services and the use of the church. Sister Joyce Anderson, the pastor's wife, supported him through the building process. Sister Anderson's commitment also increased. She became part and parcel to her husband's commitment. Sister Anderson is a wonderful compliment to her husband.

With support, St. Paul is truly a beacon in the community. Years ago, when St. Paul had limited facilities and sometimes limited people for a special task, the people in the community offered their services. That relationship brought about an informal partnership that still continues through Rev. Anderson's tenure at St. Paul.

Several years ago I received a phone call around 10:30 PM on a Friday night. The person, who called left Palmyra more than fifty years ago. She wanted Rev. Anderson to officiate her brother's funeral, who died down south after leaving Palmyra, years ago?

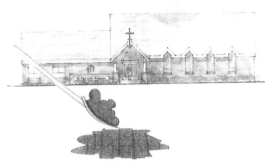

ST PAUL UAME CHURCH, PALMYRA, NEW JERSEY
REV CHARLES M. ANDERSON — PASTOR

GROUND BREAKING SERVICE
SATURDAY — AUGUST 21, 2004 — 1:00PM

THE RT REV MICHAEL S. MOULDEN - *Presiding*
PRESIDING PRELATE — 2nd, 3rd and 5th EPISCOPAL DISTRICTS
PRESIDENT OF THE BENCH OF BISHOPS
UNION AMERICAN METHODIST EPISCOPAL CHURCH, INC

ST PAUL UAME CHURCH — CHURCH CONSTRUCTION PROJECT

PROJECT OVERSIGHT

THE BUILDING COMMITTEE

Bro J. Lloyd Scott, Jr (T)   Sis Lorraine Austin (S)   Bro Charles A Pratt (T)   Bro William Roy (T)
COMM CHAIRMAN   BLDG FUND CHAIR

Bro Keith Austin (T)   Bro William Welcher (T)   Committee Advisors — The Congregation

DESIGN & DEVELOPMENT	BUILDER	FINANCING
ARCHITECTS	GENERAL CONTRACTOR	LIEN HOLDER
Lammey & Giorgio — Hadden Twp, NJ	F & H Builders, Inc — Burlington, NJ	Commerce Bank
Mr William Lammey	Mr Fred Ham	LOAN OFFICERS
Mr Sean Furlong	Mr Bill Bryant — Site Mgr	Miss Eileen Echols
		Mr Greg De Witt
COUNSEL	INSURANCE	CLOSING AGENT
ATTORNEY	HILDEBRAND AGENCY	Miss Rebecca Sherman
Earp & Cohn PC	Guide One Church Insurance	
Mr Donald Nogowski	Mr Dean Hildebrand	

Now, . . ., the LORD be with thee; and prosper thou, and
build the house of the LORD thy God, as he hath said of thee.
1 CHRONICLES 22:11

Ground Breaking Ceremony at
St. Paul Union American Methodist Episcopal Church

Lorraine Austin, Rev. Milton Brooks, Aunt Bea

Rev. Anderson, Lorraine Austin, Esther Colter,
Janet Still-Johnson, Sandra Pratt

St. Paul UAME Congregation

Men's Community Choir along with
St. Paul Baptist Church Men's Choir, Cinnaminson, NJ

She wanted the funeral on Monday morning at the local Funeral Home. She did not want the use of the church for anything. Rev. Anderson honored her wishes.

At the burial site, Rev. Anderson received a request, from the family to use the church to feed family and friends, he agreed. The family would try to get some food for about twenty people. I remember seeing Rev. Anderson take out his cell phone and talk to somebody. I think it was to Marva Jones. If you want something done, call on Marva Jones. She may step on your toes, but that goes with the territory. I call her General (Mam) Marva Jones. Shortly after we got back to the church, Marva Jones had secured enough food and troops to serve around twenty plus people in a very short time. People from St. Paul were not present to help because no one expected the church to play any part in the funeral.

In the kitchen, there were three people from St. Paul; General Marva Jones, Rev. Anderson and Private Pratt. From the community: Elaine Myers Brown, Audrey Jean Butler, Frannie Coles, Josie Grimes, Geneva Coles Pratt and Fern Quinton. Speaking of General Marva Jones, she saw me sitting down, while the others were preparing the food. Private Pratt, she shouted, get over here and cut up the roast chickens. Of course I said; yes, General Mam. My back had been hurting for a couple of days. Serving as one of the pallbearers along with Rev. Anderson, did not help my aching back. Did I say anything to General Jones about my back no, did I think she would care, no. The bottom line, we were there to serve the family and that is what we did.

St. Paul and the community coming together again. When I made a comment, that some of you, helped at my mother's funeral, held at Evergreen Baptist Church, in March of 1966. Then I heard the voice of Audrey Jean Butler, we are just one big family. The people in the neighborhood, are so proud to tell you that the one big family theory is still alive and working. The big family is even bigger, with the addition of the St. Paul family. There is a reason that some people think Rev. Anderson is the community Pastor and St. Paul the community Church. Could it be because Rev. Anderson, St. Paul, and the community share their commitment in the community?

If I hear the one big family theory again, I am going to suggest that somebody in the neighborhood, commission someone to create the following sign or plaque. "You are now entering the Neighborhood of the One Big Family". As for St. Paul, I remember when eight year old John Mark Stauffer, from my neighborhood said to me, "We are here to serve". A sign or plaque bearing those words would look good somewhere within the confines of St. Paul, just a thought. Sign or no-sign, the village better known as St. Paul U.A.M.E. Church will continue to raise those in their care and beyond.

Appendix

The following is a small sample of the people, events and conditions that created my life's memories. Naming people is difficult, as someone is always overlooked. My apologies to those I missed.

My Family

My **mom** and **dad** separated when I was 12 or 13 years old. However, I never thought of our family as dysfunctional in any way. When one of my friends at college praised me for going to college, having come from a single parent home, I looked at this person strangely. I had no idea what he was talking about. We were still a family. Our mother didn't treat us like we were the best thing since sliced bread; she had expectations for her children. As a member of the family, you had chores and there was no negotiation.

In addition to chores, we had to find some kind of job. On Saturday and Sunday, we had to be out of bed by 8 a.m. When we were old enough to caddy, we were up by 7 a.m. We could not use weather as an excuse. My mother worked for people who practically lived on the golf course. She knew when the crazies were playing golf. Fishermen and golfers always think the weather is good.

When we caddied, we earned $1.40. Most golfers would give us a 10 cent tip. Out of this money, most of us would go to the club restaurant to get a sandwich. My favorite sandwich was the liverwurst sandwich with that bright yellow mustard. Cost 20 cents. When we got home, mom took the dollar. We didn't tell her about the 10 cent tip. Even when we were strong enough to carry two bags, we didn't tell mom. The thought of carrying two bags for four hours and all you have to show for it was a dollar – Nah. My brothers and I would sometimes play cards for money one or two cents from our "salary." If you lost your money, you had to borrow back. Don't let mom come home from work and don't have her dollar.

Mom came from a family (the Cephas) of strong women, starting with **Grandmom Cephas**. There were times I thought our mother didn't love us. Having success in sports didn't change the atmosphere around the house. I could come home and say "Mom, I just won the state meet." "Good," she would say, "I want you to scrub the kitchen floor and don't forget to cover the floor with newspaper when you finish." (The papers stayed on the floor for a few days to keep it clean.)

Our mother had two dishwashers: my brother **Petey** and me. If mom wasn't around, we would argue about who was going to wash the dishes. We both wanted to dry the dishes. I don't re-member brother Merrill in the kitchen after dinner.

We had to hang washed clothes on the clothesline. In the winter, it could be brutal. Taking them down was even worse. The sheets would freeze on the line! All clothes and sheets had to be folded a certain way.

Banking the fire at night and putting coal on the fire early in the morning was another chore. To brother **Merrill**, did you know where the coal furnace or coal bin was located in the basement? Forget brother and sister **Eugene** and **Essie Mae,** they were too young and probably a little spoiled.

Mom-Mary-Audrey Pratt

Pop-Charles M. Pratt

Jillana, Jennie, Jessalyn Irons

Charles A. Pratt, Jr. - Charles A. Pratt, Sr.- Jennifer L. Pratt-Irons
and Sandra V. Person-Pratt

Alexandra, Peter, Renee & Christian Liciaga

Christian Liciaga and Ron Chambers

Ethel Mae, Charlie Pratt, Laliah Pratt and Merrill Pratt

Jackie Joyner-Kersee, Charlie and son-in-law Wayne Irons

Ethel Mae & Genie Pratt

Petey Cephas

Palmyra Giants

Grand moms Pratt and Cephas with Baby Charles A. Pratt Jr.

Gene Pratt

As tough as mom was, there was something about her that let us know we were special. She kept our modest home nice and clean. She kept both our clothes and us clean. Our meals, minus the breakfast of oatmeal and baloney sandwiches for lunch, were special. When the weather was really bad, we didn't have to go to the golf course and caddy. Saturday and Sunday breakfast was served in the dining room. Sunday dinners were always held in the dining room (tablecloths and linen napkins included). Some Sunday dinners and holidays, we had fruit cocktail before the meal and grape juice with the meal. Those holidays came with a price: polishing the silver was not an easy chore.

Mom was happy for me when I left home for college. She gave me a container to send my dirty clothes home to be washed and ironed. She sent the container back within a week. When I came home that first summer, I was in for a surprise. Mom asked me if there was a Laundromat near the college. I told her yes. Good, she said, "You won't have to send your clothes home." She taught me how to iron my shirts and press my pants. What I learned came in handy.

My dad, like many dads, was a hard worker. He did what was necessary to feed and raise a family.

I was with my dad when he gathered coal, at night, on the railroad tracks. I still have visions of him carrying a burlap bag half full of coal, his body bent over as he struggled to carry the bag to the car, hidden from view, off the road. All I had to carry was a dust pan. When we finished picking up the coal, my dad would drive uptown to buy some ice cream for the family. Picking up coal sometimes made the difference between a warm house and a cold house. Later I found out that other families had to do the same. My dad also made his own bathtub gin for sale. He would kid some customers that he took a bath in the gin before putting it in a bottle. At an early age, I was with my dad when he went to Hilton Hills to get some kind of pure white liquid. I think they had something called stills in them there hills. My dad drove his four door car into the woods. When my dad opened the back doors, someone loaded the back seat and floor with large jugs. The transfer of precious cargo didn't take long.

My dad and other fathers would shovel snow off the Tacony-Palmyra Bridge; their feet wrapped in burlap bags for warmth. (They were the snow plows)

As an adult, I asked my dad why he took me on those adventures. His reply was simply a smile – that was all the answer I needed. My father never said anything negative to me. He encouraged me to think beyond Palmyra. Most important, he had expectations for and from me.

Before I started high school, he encouraged me to spend the summers with him and his sister, **Aunt Ethel**, in Plainfield, NJ. I took his advice. The young people in Plainfield and the rest of north Jersey were talking about college. Within a day or two after arriving in Plainfield, Aunt Ethel sent me down the street to meet a family with children. They had a son my age, **William "Sonny" Wright**. Before I returned home, Sonny let me know he was going to Rutgers University and become a lawyer. When I returned home, I told Aunt Ethel what Sonny said and I didn't know what to say to him. She told me when you see him again tell him you're going to Rutgers too. Years later, I heard that Sonny Wright became a lawyer.

That summer, Aunt Ethel introduced me to the **Pettigrew family** from Roselle – mother, father and three teenage children; **Kenny**, **Blanche** and **Lillian**. All were good students. Kenny stayed with me in Plainfield. His interest in academics inspired me to think about college. He became my brother-in-law after I married his sister Blanche (the mother of my two children; **Charles Jr. (Chuck)** and **Jennifer Lynette Irons**).

Aunt Ethel introduced me to many of her friends. She took me on bus trips and various restaurants in Newark. Her work as a housekeeper for **Dr. Edward O'Brien's family** was a benefit for me. I got the job of taking care of their yard. Another benefit was the leftovers from the O'Brien family dinners. Aunt Ethel would bring the leftovers home after work. Unlike some housekeepers, the O'Briens insisted that she have dinner with them. When the O'Briens spent their summers on Nantucket Island off of Cape Cod, Massachusetts, she went with them as part of the family. I heard so much about Nantucket Island from Aunt Ethel, I wanted to see it for myself.

One summer after I started teaching school, our family visited the Cape Cod area. The Cape Cod adventure wasn't free of drama … and aroma. Somewhere on the Massachusetts Turnpike, I had car trouble, it was leaking gas. We could smell it in the car. Our children, Chuck and Jennie, were pretty young. I told them to wind down their window and be prepared to jump out if the car catches fire. I drove slowly in the right lane to conserve gas.

It was getting dark and I had no idea where we were. I was concerned about our safety and if somebody would help us. Fortunately, we made it to a truck stop. I talked to one of the mechanics about the car. He said he couldn't fix the car until the morning.

He asked where we were headed and when I gave him the information, he said he would take us to our motel and come for me when the car was finished. When I heard those words, I thought, there are good people in this world.

As we were headed to our motel, I kept seeing signs on some motels for heated pool. That meant nothing to me.

The next morning, the gentleman came to get me as promised. Driving back to the motel, again I saw those heated pool signs. Nothing registered.

When I pulled into the motel, Chuck and Jennie were sitting on the side of the pool in their bathing suits. They told me the water was great and that I should get my bathing suit and come in. I obeyed my children and came right back. They told me not to walk into the pool but to dive in from the high diving board. I obeyed my children.

When I dove in and hit the water, I instantly realized what the signs for a heated pool meant. The water was so cold it took my breath away. When I came up, those two juvenile delinquents were nowhere to be found. One of these days, I'll return the favor to Chuck and Jennie. Maybe I can get some help from Chuck's children; **Juanelle**, **Charles III** and **Joel**. Jennie's children, **Jillana** and **Jessalyn Irons** might also enjoy pulling a prank on their mother with my help.

People in Palmyra

A pillar in the community and St. Paul UAME Church, **Mr. George Cherry** was a great role model, businessman and farmer who made good use of his truck. Sometimes he would use his truck to haul trash. Other times, he would use the truck to haul spoiled fruits and vegetables from the supermarket to the local dump. Mr. George knew that some of the food was still good; he would set those items aside for us. Those of us who knew his routine would meet him at the dump. Palmyra had a very good semipro baseball team called the Palmyra Giants. With a cleaning, the truck was used to transport some of the players to away games. There was always room on the truck for the young people. As a farmer, if you wanted a job, he would find something for you to do.

Uncle Bob (Robert Young) was way ahead of his time. A contractor who built his own house, a sportsman, and most of all, a man who refused to let people set boundaries for him. He took some of his nephews and his sons, **Sonny** and **Sidney** to the Sportsman's Show at Convention Hall in Philadelphia when very few, if any, African-Americans ventured to these types of events. Apparently he crossed a boundary with someone because one morning he woke up to a burning cross on his lawn. He owned a cabin and a boat somewhere near Tuckerton. I remember when I was young; Uncle Bob took us to a tavern on Broad and Market Streets. We sat in the corner sipping soda as he sat at the bar. I had my first hot dog with onions with Uncle Bob.

After building a swimming pool for the **Smith family** outside of our neighborhood, he made it possible for us for the first time to swim in a pool. That experience was both good and bad,

Terrell Person, Don Hornick, Merrill Pratt, and Charlie Pratt

New Old-Timers

William "Bill" Cosby, Charlie Pratt and Josh Culbreath

The Pratt's and Elaine Myers

Kathy Pratt and fiancé Mike Pearson

Pratt Family Gathering

Pratt Family Gathering

because we later had to return to the filthy Pennsauken Creek to cool off. In the pool, we could see our feet – that was a different experience. In the Pennsauken Creek, we couldn't see our hands just a foot below the water level.

He took a group of us deer hunting in our early teens. We stayed in his unheated cabin overnight. Most of us had never shot a shotgun; we definitely didn't have a hunting license. After taking a practice shot with my gun, I prayed that we didn't see a deer. My prayers were answered. That practice shot jarred my shoulder.

When my friend **Billy King** was old enough to drive legally, he bought a 1929 Ford. He took several of us down to Uncle Bob's cabin. We stayed overnight. **Eddie Grimes** and I decided to sleep on Uncle Bob's boat. Sometime in the dark of night, the tide started coming in and the boat started to rock. Both of us tried to be brave. We left the boat and told the guys in the cabin the mosquitoes were so bad we had to come in.

When we got up in the morning, the car had a flat tire. We didn't have a jack. Someone found a five gallon can filled with concrete. Billy's car was very light in weight. Some of us lifted the car, and someone put the can under the car. After Billy changed the tire and we were ready to leave, Billy simply drove the car right off the five gallon can. I liked that car; a couple of dollars would fill up the gas tank. If you sat in the front passenger seat, there was nothing between you and the road but a ½ inch piece of plywood. You could lift up the floor board and see the red hot manifold and the road.

Ogden John Pratt (Uncle Buss) my father's brother, a great athlete, and a father of seven sons, many of whom inherited his athletic skills: Herbert, Lawrence **(Baldy)**, **Charles John (Bozo)**, **Leonard (Sandy)**, **Norman Davis**, **Wayne Chin** and **Robin Pratt**.

Uncle Buss was a great semi-pro football and baseball player and a great swimmer. He and **Billy Myers**, for recreation, would swim across the Delaware River and back. This stern taskmaster wasn't satisfied with keeping his swimming skills to himself. He thought his sons, nephews and their friends needed to learn survival skills in the water.

Down to the filthy Pennsauken creek behind the Meadow-brook we went, fully clothed with our bathing suit as our underwear, as ex-First Sergeant Pratt shouted out instructions to jump off the railroad bridge one at a time, and before you surface take everything off except your bathing suit. Tie your pants and shirt in a way that they become a floating aide. Put your socks in your shoes, tie your shoes together and hang them around your neck. When we surfaced, we were somewhere downstream from where we jumped in. All of us who participated passed the test.

Recently our former mailman, **Chuck Gravener**, told me that his father worked with a Pratt at Camden Lime Company in Camden many years ago. He said this Pratt guy used to swim across the Delaware River and back. That guy is my uncle, I said. Small world.

Other Special Palmyra Villagers

My choice to acknowledge these people or events may seem trivial, but they are important to me.

- **Mrs. Fannie Myers** – in addition to the fact that her son **Ernest** and I were classmates, she always had that wonderful smile. That smile represented what the community thought about its young people. That smile said to me: I know you are not my child, but I still care about you. Always great to see her sitting on the porch with her mother.

- **Mom Person** delivered me and three other siblings. I spent a lot of time at her home. Who would know that I would someday marry her granddaughter, **Sandra Person**.

- **Aunt Molly Lewis**, Mom Person's sister, one of our babysitters.

- The **George King family**, great neighbors. As a young child, I was unable to walk for a couple of days due to a mysterious ailment. **Mr. King and Mr. Tom Allen** came to our house on Jefferson Street and rubbed my legs with something they made. In a day or two, I was up and walking again. If family members had a cold or whooping cough, they made some kind of mustard rub to rub on your chest. Parents would wrap your upper body with some kind of cloth. My parents must have been part Egyptian; they wrapped us like a mummy. The smell of the mustard rub was so bad, I can still smell it.

My parents' home remedies were common in our home. If you had a toothache – mom got a hot iron and a towel and put it to your face. Need a tooth pulled? Dad went to his medical (tool) box and got his pliers … like magic, the tooth was gone and the Tooth Fairy was cheap. I am glad we didn't have any serious health problems. I hate to think what our parents' might have subjected us to.

- The **Herbert Austin family** also great neighbors. **Mr. Austin** was a nice low-profile man and his son **Herbert** (Gabe) was a carbon copy. Gabe ran the half mile in high school. He made it look so easy. The first time I saw a chicken run around with its head cut off, it belonged to Mr. Austin.

- The **Wilbon family** always willing to help when mom needed to borrow a cup of sugar, flour or butter. I told my mom that I liked Aunt Daisy's cornbread better than hers. That was not cool. Aunt Daisy was Mom Person's daughter.

- The **Hinson family** our cousins. It was -great to have our cousins close by. **Aunt Lucille**, my mother's sister, was one of those strong Cephas women probably tougher than mom. Having cousins **Elmer** and **James** close by was fun. We were together every day. Cousins **Doris, Mary Ann, Albert, George** and **Louise** were younger but they brought joy to the

Cephas/Hinson/Pratt clan. Aunt Lucille and mom were together all the time. When they talked about the soap operas on the radio, I thought they were talking about real people.

- The **Kelly family** moved down to Jefferson Street and brought some class with them. Daughters **Jacqueline**, **Valeria**, and **Naomi**, and sons **Fred**, **William**, **Charles** and **Lawrence** were an asset to the neighborhood.

- The **Jack Johnson family** pillars in the community. **Mrs. Johnson** was a community activist and faithful member at St. Paul UAME Church. Who could forget **Aunt Bea**? She was a role model for girls interested in sports. She made wonderful flower arrangements for St. Paul and was an asset to the senior choir.

- The **Claude Young family**; a businessman; wife, a wonderful sweet lady with five daughters; **Eleanor**, **Carolyn**, **Jo Ann**, **Yvonne** and **Claudia**.

- **Honey Lindsay** was a wonderful neighbor. She had a phone and we didn't. She gladly shared her phone with us.

- **Mrs. Farrell Lindsay** always pleasant and kind. Never got any of her candy she used to give out.

- The **Gilcrist family** had no children. Every Easter, we went to their house to make eggnog. Mr. Gilcrest would hire me when he had odd jobs to do. I think our parents hid the Christmas toys at their house.

- The **Jim King Family** – who could forget **Lefty**, **Beaty**, **Brenda**, **Diane** and **Chucky**? Lefty was a great baseball player.

- The **John Johnson family** owned a tailor shop. I delivered clothes for them. Lived in a signature house on Market Street. Nice family.

- The **Scott family** came to Palmyra from Virginia. Brought with them southern hospitality. **Lloyd** was a role model, a great football player and a pillar at St. Paul Church. He has a brother and two sisters; **Geraldine** my classmate and **Yvonne**. I can't remember Lloyd's brother's name.

- The **Shelly King family** – **Mr. King** a part of a group of colored soldiers that fought in World War I in France. He survived the war, but incurred nerve damage when the enemy used poison gas against his company. He returned home but carried the unpleasant effects of the poison gas to his grave.

- The **Dr. Hardy family** – the community was proud to have a black doctor living among them.

- The **John Cauthorne family** – **Mr. Cauthorne** stopped me one day coming home from school with my head hanging low. I had just finished last, again, in a track meet. From that day as a freshman in high school, until his death, he continued to encourage me. I enjoy my talks with **Mrs. Cauthorne** (Marion) and their daughter **Barbara**.

- The **Elwood Young family** – **Mr. Young** my mentor. When he had errands to do, he would come to our house and get me. He continued to support me and sing my praises until his death. He was a great athlete and musician who receive part of his education at the Bordentown Manual Training School Institute. His son, Brother is one of the good guys out of Palmyra. I made sure he knew how much his father meant to me. His dad was the only one in Palmyra who thought I could play football.

- The house of **Grandmom Pratt**, my father's mother, was our second home. Every day after breakfast, minus schools days, we went straight to Grandmom's house. Grandmom was special to all of her grandchildren.

- The **Bob Young family** – There is some truth that opposites attract. **Uncle Bob** and **Aunt Hazel**, my father's sister, couldn't be any more opposite. She was known for her class and dignity. Uncle Bob was a rebel who probably didn't own a suit or tie. Cousins **Sonny**, **Sidney** and **Janet** must have fallen out of Uncle Bob's tree. The Young's house, built by Uncle Bob, didn't look like our house. Beautiful hardwood floors; eight-inch trim around the floors, finished in a natural stain; antiques and colonial furniture ... Sidney's Lionel train set in their large basement, a source of envy. A beautiful house for a collection of characters. Brother Merrill and Sidney spent a lot of time together growing up. Now they blame each other for their errant behavior. I think they went to New York in a car to a nightclub around the age of fifteen. I think Sidney was driving the car. Please tell me I am wrong.

- The **Horace Still family** a great example of family unity. Who could forget big #33, **Ken Still**? **Janet Johnson** and her cousin **Barbara Cherry** were early role models. Both graduated from college and became educators. Janet is a great contributor to St. Paul UAME Church in Palmyra and to the UAME Church Conference.

- The **Flournoy family** included one of our great role models, Tee-Wee Flournoy. He became the first black chief of police in a predominately-white community. Great source of pride for the neighborhood.

- The **Smith family** – **Mr. Lloyd Smith** a junk man who would buy your junk. Good family members; one of his sons, **Sam (Junkie) Smith**, took over his father's business.

- The **Sam Austin family** – You just knew they were an important family in the community. Daughter **Evelyn** followed my career when she lived in North Jersey. Son **Joe** always had something positive to say to me.

- The **Blaine Ridgway family** – **Mr. Ridgway** and my father occasionally worked together. When I visited their work site on Market Street in Palmyra, Mr. Ridgway would teach me math time's tables and compliment me when I got the right answer. His daughter **Phyllis** (Scott) a great contributor to St. Paul. She and her husband, **Lloyd Scott**, have served St. Paul UAME Church over 50 years.

- The **Merrill Johns family** good friends. We enjoyed their collection of sons and daughters.

- **Mr. Jim Folks** another family friend; he was a journeyman barber. He would cut your hair in his yard or come to your house. He would supply our family with wild rabbits.

- The **Poppa Coles family** great people. I enjoyed growing up with the Coles family children. Daughter **Mickey** and I were classmates. **Frannie** and **Geneva** (Gin) great asset to the Austin Singers. Both continue to serve the community

- The **Johnny Myers family** lived so close to my cousins,

I thought of them as family. When part of their family moved to Elizabeth, I would visit them. **Elaine** and **Marva** are great contributors to the community. I always looked for Elaine when she worked at the Moorestown Mall. Marva does a great job of decorating St. Paul UAME Church.

- The **Allen family** on Third Street, a gracious family. On our way home from school, we were always invited into their home for goodies.

- "**Villari**" the smell of fresh baked Italian rolls traveled two or three blocks. For two cents, they were the best rolls in the world. Can you imagine what the rolls taste like with butter?

When I grew up on Jefferson and Front Streets, I heard stories about the people who lived on Fourth, Fifth and Sixth Streets. They were labeled the "upper crust" of the neighborhood, the people whose names would be listed in the social registry if there was such a thing.

In some areas of the world, the higher you lived in the mountains, the higher your status. Palmyra doesn't have any mountains, but the streets for the most part were listed in numerical order. If you lived below Fourth Street, you were a "Downtowner." That included Market, Jefferson, Horseshoe Bend, and Washington (now Kennedy) Streets. If you lived on Fourth, Fifth or Sixth streets you were an "Uptowner." That included Arch, Race and Legion Streets.

Some downtowners were convinced that the Uptowners had it better than them. As a Downtowner, I wondered why some of the Uptowners went to church in Riverton. Some of us viewed

Riverton as upscale with an elite mentality. That perception is still alive in my mind, but I don't see it as a social problem. (Sorry, Iris Gaughan) Like the dreaded railroad tracks, some may use location in a town or neighborhood as a status symbol. There was no real separation in our neighborhood, though, because we were all in the same boat. The issues that plagued our community didn't stop at Third Street. Like most Urban Myths and Legends, the truth lies somewhere between truth and fiction.

The following families played a prominent role in our community. They happened to live above Third Street.

- The family of **Mr. Trim Austin**, daughters, **Willa**, **Helen** and **Mary**.

- The **Grimes family**; **Percy** and **Eddie** were my teammates.

- **Mr. Johnny Williams**;

- **Mr. Stevenson**;

- The **Robert Hunter family**, daughters **Helen** and **Doris**;

- **Mr. Joe Conwell**;

- The **Wilbur Johnson family** – **Mr. Johnson** and **Mr. Mumford Ruffin**, the man who built our house in Moorestown, were great friends. Many times Mr. Johnson came to see what progress we were making on the house; sometimes he came with trees, shrubs and flowers.

- The **Doc Hunt family**; **Ella Mae** (my classmate), **Harry**, **Lynch**, **Doc**, **Sam** and **Heddi**.

- **Lola Jane Hunt's Family**;

- The **Berkhead family** on Race Street.

- The **John Poindexter family**—always good to see **John**, a lawyer.

- The **Dorsey family**; Great people, starting with the parents. All the boys: **Bill**, **Alfred** (Duke), **Robert**, **Max** and **Al** (Brown) were special.

- The **Richard Ruffin family**; I remember son **Dick** and always looked for daughter **Geraldine**, who worked at Sears.

- All those **Washingtons**: **Victor**, **John**, **Howard**, **Billy**, **Wilbur** and **Mrs. Edna Washington Webb**. The Washingtons are very much admired in Palmyra and beyond.

Victor was a good person and family man; he was an early mentor to Terrell (Terry) Person. John was committed to making all of Palmyra a good place to live. He was one of the first to call me Charles Arthur. I had something in common with Howard – we both enjoyed working in the yard. Billy (William) was an officer in the Army. That alone made him a great role model. After Wilbur left Palmyra when I was in grade school, I had a hard time catching up with him. Then I read about this esteemed pastor named Wilbur Washington. Recently I got to know him again and his wife, Marie Hunt Washington. When I am with him, I tell him he is my favorite Washington. When I see John, I tell him he's my favorite. But neither is true – my favorite is their sister, –Mrs. Edna, I saved the best for last. Mrs. Edna Washington Webb. She is prim and proper in stature with perfect diction. Sometimes she calls my name so proper, I don't know who she is referring to. However, when you get to know her, you find out she is really down to earth.

One day I saw a new house being built on Sixth Street. I wondered who was building the house. Were they one of us? They must have money.

Someone told me **Nathaniel "Pete" Person** and his wife

Lillian, were having the house built. I knew all the Person brothers except for Pete. Not a good testimony on my part, Pete Person would eventually become my father-in-law. My future mother-in-law Lillian was known for her fried chicken, oven-baked spare ribs and stuffed fish. Her fried chicken traveled as far as Germany and Japan thanks to her granddaughter **Renee**, who was performing in those countries. Having a house built on Sixth Street by someone who grew up in the last house downtown was impressive.

After the Person's built their house, I went off to college. It would be years later before I engaged someone on the social status of my home neighborhood. If I harbored any slight notion that the four, five or six hundreds label was still alive, I would be mistaken. Welcome to the new reality.

Brother **Merrill** and wife **Katherine** moved to Sixth Street. **Dickie King** also lived on Sixth Street. My future brother in-law, **Terrell Person**. The esteemed pastor of the historic Jacob's Chapel in Mt. Laurel, and his sister, my future wife Sandra, grew up on Sixth Street. Could these people be considered part of the socially elite? I doubt it. With mentors like Uncle Bob Young, Merrill Pratt, my dad and Richard "Dickie Kush" King, Terrell Person didn't have a chance to get his name in the factitious social register.

When I became part of the Person family, Lil's kitchen was open to this former downtowner. Miss Lil's signature dishes lived up to their reputation. Sandra's dad would always kid me about spending more time at his kitchen table than he did. During some family get together the subject of social class would be revisited. Terrell and Sandra (not Terry and Sandy) would declare their royal upbringing. Sandra's father said she had visions of being the Queen of Sheba, the ancient Queen of Egypt. What is a father to think, he gave his teenage daughter enough money to buy a complete Easter Outfit and she spent all of it on one garment? If Dickie King who lived on 6th Street preferred to be called Kush, after an ancient King in Africa why can't Sandra have visions of royalty? Terrell is not above declaring his royal upbringing when he wants to get a reaction out of me.

I admire what Terrell has done as pastor of Jacob's Chapel, in Mt. Laurel NJ. His mentoring program in the Mt. Laurel school system, his summer camp for young people and his Church's food pantry that supports Burlington County are highly praised in the community and beyond. His commitment goes beyond those much needed programs.

All of his success comes with a price I don't like. He gets his name and picture in the paper too much! People see me and say, "I know you; you're Pastor Person's brother in-law." When will this stop? I went through the same thing with my brothers Merrill and Gene and my sister Essie Mae (real name Ethel Mae). Everyone knew me only as so and so's brother. Even my cousin, Charles John Bozo Pratt, was part of my lost identity. Back in high school, when I earned a state Championship medal, guess whose initials are on the medal? Not C.A.P. but C.J.P.

It got so bad that a newspaper thought I was two people. My full name is Charles Arthur ("Artie") Pratt. In Palmyra, you are only recognized by your nickname (Artie). The newspaper recognized Charles Pratt for winning the decathlon and his cousin Artie for starting the Pratt tradition in sports – but both were me.

Several years ago, brother Merrill accused Cousin Sidney and me of being five hundreds and we don't live in Palmyra. He would tell people that I cut my grass in a three piece suit. I hate it when people exaggerate about me. The truth is I never cut my grass in a three piece suit, only a two piece suit. Some people think I don't have any old clothes (Laliah Pratt). That's not true. Her grandfather buys some of his clothes at Flea Markets. Sometimes they are too big for him. I buy them to work in the yard. How could Sidney be upper crust with a father named Bob Young?

Down Memory Lane (For the Palmyra Folks)

- Our neighborhood had their special Fourth of July activities, in addition to the ones uptown and Riverton Park. Block parties were a great source of joy. Street races were a daily occurrence and Nooni King was the fastest around. She would beat anyone who dared to come down to Jefferson Street; that included the boys.

- I have to admit: **Bugs Lindsey**, **Katherine Pratt** (my sister in-law) and **Geraldine Scott** are among those who beat me running. Bugs is one of the good guys in town. Katherine will probably put it on Facebook or something. Geraldine has been kind to me, a great classmate.

- Brother **Gene**, **Dickie King** and **Bobby Ross** from East Riverton were good street runners. Later, when Gene was working as a car salesman, he was challenged by a younger salesman (**Alan Gorman**) to race on the car lot. Gene, in his dress clothes, beat Alan. Since then Alan has sold me my last four cars.

- In talking with **Ronald Catlett**, I found that he opened his home to his son's college friends. I remember my college days.

- To prove your toughness in Palmyra, guys had to play football in the Dust Bowl: Tackle football on a dusty field with no equipment for protection. It was Downtown against Uptown.

Playing in the Dust Bowl was good, but some of us wanted to play on a real football field. Since there was no little league football, some of us went over to the stadium, climbed the fence and planned our strategy. Part of our strategy was to gain access to the equipment room. It's a secret how we got all the equipment. Partially or fully equipped, with uniforms, we played on the high school's football field. After the game we returned all of the equipment to the equipment room, minus a few t-shirts.

Our behavior that afternoon earned us a visit to the local court. Never found out who reported the football game and names to the police. When the police knocked on the door at our house, I was there to greet them. I was shocked when they told me I had to meet with the Justice of the Peace, Judge Stone. Unknown to some of us Uncle Bob Young and Uncle Bobby Person were in court, as well. The Judge talked to us and our parents about our errant behavior. When he finished, Uncle Bob Young and Uncle Bobby Person (all 6'4" of him) asked for permission to address the bench. I don't know what those two characters with giant personalities said to the judge, but it had to be good. Justice Stone didn't impose any penalties on us. Uncle Bob and Uncle Bobby talked to us about our behavior before we went home.

- Who could forget the Meadowbrook in Palmyra, a famous dance hall that attracted people from south Jersey and

Philadelphia? Live music and the latest dance steps was the norm.

Mr. Monk Ruffin, the builder and owner of the Meadow-brook, brought joy to a lot of people. On occasion, students from LaSalle College in Philadelphia would rent the dance hall for private parties.

- Our community had several speakeasies and after-hours places. Some folks called them private clubs. Our age group was too young to frequent those places, but we knew all about them. One of the most famous speakeasies was Duffy's Tavern. For more information on Duffy's Tavern, ask **Ty Belford**.

Our family lived in the house that became Duffy's Tavern long before the Belfords occupied it. Men would come to our house and for 10 cents they would get a small shot glass, one or two ounces of White Lighting. As a youngster, I couldn't understand why someone would drink something that would cause them to make such a horrible face. In our backyard, we had a pond filled with water and maybe some fish. The pond was my dad's prized possession. When he got a tip that the cops were going to raid the private "club" (our house), he hid the bottles of "ice tea" in the pond.

- **Jobie Cooper** was our outdoorsman. How good it was, having our very own Tarzan in our community. He was a hunter, trapper and fisherman. He was one of the people who brought the muskrat, a river rodent that lived in the marshes, to our dinner table. When my mother got finished cooking this delicacy, we didn't care what it was or where it came from. After my mother passed on, I lost my taste for both rabbits and muskrat.

My mother was a good cook, but some dishes I could have

done without. Her kidney stew is one, and chitterlings (small intestines of pigs), another. Once a year, usually Easter Sunday, we would have a leg of lamb with mint jelly. Lamb dishes were rare in our neighborhood.

- One of my greatest memories as a child was spending Sundays at **Grandmom Cephas**' house in Haddonfield. Grandmom Cephas was my mother's mother. My mother was one of 13 children. Most of my aunts and uncles were present for the Sunday dinner. The total for Sunday's dinner could easily exceed 25 people every Sunday. It was great having the Hinson, Butler and Dansbury cousins present. Some of our cousins became outstanding athletes. Both **Billy** and **David Hinson Griggs** played in the National Football League after stellar careers at the University of Virginia.

That Sunday experience was what I considered the heart and soul of a village. Grown-ups coming together to act in the best interest of all the children present. There was something about Grandmom C. that commanded respect. She didn't say much, but she communicated with her body language. She looked at you and you got the message. Behave, or you will have to deal with me.

All of Grandmom's adult children, and I suspect sons and daughters in-law, addressed her with reverence. It was always, "yes ma'am" or "no ma'am." Never yes or no.

- Once a year, Grandmom would kill or have someone kill a large pig. From that pig, she would make homemade scrapple, the best in the world. The only problem with a large family was that each family received only one to two pounds of scrapple to take home. Our lot didn't go far in our home. Since my child-hood, I have tried to find scrapple close to Grandmom's scrapple. No luck.

- Several years after we started going to Grandmom C's for Sunday dinner, another family event occurred. My mother start-ed having a family gathering at our house on July 4. Two great events came out of this family gathering: homemade ice cream and our football game in the backyard. We had an old manual ice cream maker, the one you used rock salt and had to turn the handle for a number of minutes. The result was about a quart of ice cream for over twenty people. There was no shortage of help when it came to making more ice cream.

- Our family football games had one special player, **Aunt Frances**. She thought she was Mean Joe Green (of course, Joe Green was not around at that time). Aunt Frances looked like she got pleasure when she hit you hard.

Aunt Etta didn't play in the football game. She was calm and gentle. She was the only aunt I wasn't afraid of. Aunt Etta makes a great three layered coconut cake. However, she has never tasted one of those cakes. Would you trust a slim cook who wouldn't eat his/her own food? Love and trust you, Aunt Etta!

There was no possibility that **Aunt Catherine** played in the football game. It is hard to imagine that "Miss Fashion Plate," with her well-coiffed hair, stylish clothes and fancy shoes would play with a group of rag-a-muffins. I believe **Aunt Geneva** played in those games. She could put a hurting on you.

What I really remember about Aunt Geneva is how she put her life on hold when my mother got sick.

The day my mother got sick, I had left Riverside High School and stopped at my mother's house to change into my bridge uniform. I told her I would be back for dinner. It was the same ritual for all the days I worked part-time at the bridge. When I returned for dinner, the house was empty but my dinner was prepared and wrapped on a plate. I sensed something was wrong.

In a few minutes, my cousin **Herbie Pratt** came to the house and told me that mom had a stroke and was hospitalized. All of my mother's sisters pitched in after that, but Aunt Geneva spent many hours at our house. Aunt Geneva even got me to do something my mother couldn't make me do. I never ate my mother's chitterlings and hog maws (parts of a pig). When Aunt Geneva was taking care of mom, she cooked some and I ate them for the first time, and yes, they were good. Cousin **Loretta Bruce** reminds me of her mother, Aunt Geneva.

- In my senior year, our football team played Haddonfield. My cousin **Elmer Hinson** and I played for Palmyra. Our **Uncle Billy Cephas**, who was younger than us, played for Haddonfield. This gifted all-around athlete led his team to victory. Never trust your relatives; Uncle Billy scored two touchdowns on me.

- My mother rented a room in our house to some of the people from the neighborhood. I learned something from each of the following borders.

- **Tom Allen**, one of the community's storytellers, taught me something about the history of Palmyra. I also learned that he was part of the historic Black Army division that served with distinction in Italy during World War II.

- **Billy Myers** was a great role model. Had a good work ethic.

Took care of himself and his car. Always said encouraging things to me. Came to New York to see me compete in Madison Square Garden.

- **Mr. & Mrs. Charles Nick Syers**; he was one of the real characters in the town. Convinced the family that muskrat was a delicacy. We believed him. His wife, Miss Mabel, was very fond of her dog, Snookie. He ate better than us.

- **Uncle John Person and family**. They were almost invisible. They stayed to themselves. When they came down stairs, they were a joy to be with. Uncle John always made me feel good about myself. Uncle John and Sandra's father were brothers.

Years ago my father said, good things never go out of style. To the good people of Palmyra, your neighborhood may have experienced some changes over the years. Your core values have never changed. Don't let those changes rob you of the things that are dear to you. Don't abandon the family and neighborhood traditions that made the neighborhood one big family.

People at Manhattan College

There were many important people while I was at Manhattan College, including:

- **Bob English**, fellow Hall of Famer. A key person on the mile and two mile relay teams. More important, he and his wife **Patsy** had several socials at their home for teammates. I spent a wonderful weekend at their home after a Hall of Fame affair. That weekend I wore a ragged sweat suit and a pair of slippers worse than my sweat suit. My granddaughter, **Aleah Blue Chambers**, used to tease me about how bad my slippers looked. I wore those ugly garments hoping Bob would be embarrassed and buy me something new. No luck. He had a special pair of cuff links I was hoping he would give to me. No luck again. However, when my church held a fundraiser for a new church, twice he was more than generous.

- **Richard Simmons**, a fellow Hall of Famer, was called on to compete in events outside of his comfort level. Had several parties at his house to bring the track guys together. He was proud of his teammates. We spent quality time together until his passing. He is missed.

- **Al Larsen** was more than a teammate, he was a friend; a good guy with a great work ethic.

- **The Lucas brothers**, **Roy** and **Dr. Ronald Lucas**, were both contributors to the mile relay team. Both continued to follow my career after college.

- **Tom Lindgren**, a fellow Hall of Famer; a senior member on the team, a solid person, dependable when needed. Partners at several golf outings. I miss him.

- **Bill St. Clair**, fellow Hall of Famer; before I met him, I was told he was a good cross country runner and half miler. He changed my thinking about people of color running cross country. Good friend, sorely missed.

- **Steve Dillon**, Hall of Famer, threw the 35 pound weight. He gave some depth to our weight events. Always smiling and personable.

- **Ken Bantum**, Hall of Famer and member of the 1956 Olympic team as a shot putter. Scored many points for Manhattan in the shot put and discus; some in the hurdles. Ken was also a member of our shuttle hurdles team that won at the Penn Relays. This 6'5", 230 lb. athlete thrilled the stadium; when he ran the second leg in the shuttle hurdles relay, he gave us the lead.

- **Dr. Louis Knight** – I visited his home in Jamaica several times. He was gracious to a fault. My chief competitor in the hurdles. Great host and Hall of Famer.

- **Bob Goodwin** didn't have a big profile when he came to Manhattan. Through hard work, he became a valuable member on the two mile relay team.

- **Bob Sbarra**, Hall of Famer; winner of the two mile race at the Penn Relays.

- **Frank Gaffney**, a high jumper who gave the team needed points in the field events. Made you feel good when your spirits were low.

- **Lenny Moore**, Hall of Famer. Great all-around performance. Long jumper, sprinter and member of several relay teams.

- **Wally Pina**, Hall of Famer, a solid contributor to the mile relay teams.

- **Bill Lucas**, a distance runner who earned points in events requiring great conditioning.

My Neighbors

Besides my immediate neighbors, I would like to acknowledge some of the people (and their families) that I have spent quality time with.

- **Robin** and **Rick Pleuse** showed me how great neighbors can be. On a sunny day in February 2009, I decided to wash my car. Rick decided to walk their dog around the block. When he saw me washing my car, he hollered to me, "Old man, what are you doing in New Jersey in the cold weather, aren't you retired?" I joked that I had made plans to go to Jamaica for a week in March. He told me he could make me a better offer, and offered me access to his family condo in Sarasota, Florida. I stayed three weeks.

- Thanks to Robin and Rick, I was able to spend time with two other friends in Florida. I visited **Christine** and **Richard Boucher**, a couple from our neighborhood before moving to Florida. Over a cup of coffee, we enjoyed talking about traveling. When friends of theirs from Ireland came over for a visit, I enjoyed having lunch with the group.

- The second family really consider me a part of their family. They are my son-in-law's (**Wayne Irons**) sister and husband, **Alicia and Craig Matheson**. They live in Orlando. The couple, both employed by Disney, call me Pop-Pop. They spoiled me when they made it possible for me to enjoy Disney World and Epcot. I enjoyed dinners with them and their friends. Their beautiful home was open to me.

Age has some benefits. Alicia looked after me like my daughter Jennie. Craig was not so kind to me – when we played golf, he took no mercy on me. It took me two shots to reach his drive and I was driving from the senior tees. A year later, he scored a hole in one. However, Craig's father can hold his own against him. I look forward to seeing Craig's parents again, especially his dad on the golf course.

- **Carol** and **Joe** (**Chick**) **Mauro** have opened their home to me. Chick and I walk together on occasion. His son, Joe, was always available if I needed help lifting heavy objects. When Chick visits Joe, who moved down the shore, sometimes I go with him. The three of us enjoy finding good eateries.

- Our former mailman, **Chuck Gravener**, lives nearby and makes you feel good about the people in the larger neighborhood. Chuck is just a good guy.

- **Derrick DeSliva** lives in the subdivision in back of our house. I enjoy talking with him. He is people friendly.

- In 2004, while walking around the lake about a quarter mile from our house, I met a fellow named **Joe Bryski**. Joe and I have had many talks since then. I think of Joe as a good friend. Whenever Joe knows that someone is in need of something, he tries to fill that need. He takes great pride his neighborhood. His wife **Diane** always has a hello when I see her. They both marvel how fast my wife walks around the lake in the back of their yard. Some of the neighbors around the lake swear that they hear her talking to the wildlife around the lake (and they would be right).

- **Joe Derillo**, a high school classmate of Joe Bryski and lives in the same neighborhood, is one of the good guys. If he sees me walking and he's driving his car, he stops to say hello. When we run into each other, I always enjoy our talks.

While walking around the lake, I met a special couple, **Rochelle** and **Fred Alicea**. After the Aliceas opened their home to me, I found that Fred knew a lot about my hometown Palmyra. He used to work for Verizon. We know some of the same people.

Rochelle retired as a teacher from the Camden school system. Fred, an ex-basketball player, now a pool shark, is waiting to beat me in pool, but I won't give him a chance. I was at his house when his father in-law and several friends were there for a friendly game of pool. There was so much trash talking during the pool games I thought the neighbors might call the police. The trash talking continued during a late lunch. Fred couldn't wait to get back to the pool table and beat someone.

Fred has no respect for his elders – he calls me old man, even though he has more gray hair than I do. Fred won't tell this story, but I will: his neighbors across the street saw the two of us walking and asked Fred if I was his son.

Sometimes, Fred and I walk around the lake. I take it easy on him because some of these younger guys have fragile egos. Sometimes when I am walking around the lake, I find Fred fishing; I think that's what he calls it. Believe me, the fish in the lake are not in any danger.

After 30 years of people moving in and out of the neighborhood, it still remains a good place to live. I continue to see value in the people in the neighborhood. It started with David Mosca. He shaped my thinking about people. After David came John Mark Stauffer, another young person. He strengthened my feelings of the goodness of people.

Years later, some other young people in the neighborhood made me believe that society in general is moving forward, not backwards. **Sarah** and **Nicolas Delio** always speak with me when they walk past our house. Sarah always waves when she goes pass in the family van. **Terri Purdy**, her brother Jim, and Angelica

Baranek always greet me with a, "Hello, Mr. Pratt." Angelica may greet me and wife several times a day, always with a happy face. She has a special bond with my wife.

Some years ago, **Cynthia** and **David Sobel's** young daughter, **Angela**, offered to help me shovel snow. Of course, I declined the help. However, I appreciated the offer.

With a number of people in the neighborhood as good as these people, friendly and caring, what's not to like about the neighborhood?

As mentioned in the One Man Village-Milt Campbell we have remained friends throughout the years. There are frequent phone calls with a lot of laughter and kidding one another of our past athletic accomplishments.

Last year I shared with Milt that I was writing a book and included a chapter about him and our relationship that had developed between us over the years. Milt was anxious to read that chapter and I am glad he did because he did not live to read the entire book.

Linda Rusch, Campbell's partner of 13 years, reported to the Associated Press, Milt died Friday, November 4, 2012 at his home in Gainesville, about 55 miles northwest of Atlanta. She said he had been fighting prostate cancer for a decade.

''He was extremely disciplined,'' Rusch told The Associated Press on Saturday. ''He had huge passion. For you to win the gold you have to be so self-motivated and so self-disciplined. And you have to have a very strong mind.''

''He literally had to train himself to have this incredible mind, to be such a positive thinker,'' she added. ''He carried that way of life throughout his whole entire being.''

Who is Charlie Pratt?
8th grade photo, top row, second from the right.

CPSIA information can be obtained at www.ICGtesting.com
Printed in the USA
LVOW01s0413170114

369832LV00010B/24/P